SECOND EDITION

LONGMAN

ESL

LITERACY

STUDENT BOOK

YVONNE WONG NISHIO

Evans Community Adult School
Los Angeles Unified School District

Longman

Longman ESL Literacy Student Book, Second Edition

Pearson Education, 10 Bank Street, White Plains, NY 10606

Senior acquisitions editor: Allen Ascher
Development editor: Jessica Miller
Production editors: Helen Ambrosio/Linda Moser
Cover design: Curt Belshe
Text design adaptation: Page Designs
Text composition: Page Designs
Text art: Jill Wood, Stuart Iwasaki

Library of Congress Cataloging-in-Publication Data

Nishio, Yvonne Wong.
    Longman ESL literacy student book / Yvonne Wong Nishio. – 2nd ed.
      p.   cm.
    ISBN 0-201-35182-X
    1. English language – Textbooks for foreign speakers.   2. Readers
for new literates.   I. Title.
PE1128.N57   1998
428.2'4 – dc21   97-46997
                                                       CIP

13 14 15 - CRS - 0706

CONTENTS

INTRODUCTION

The Second Edition of LONGMAN ESL LITERACY is now even easier to teach! With more opportunities for oral interaction, basic grammar models, clearer instruction lines, and an expanded TEACHER'S RESOURCE BOOK, LONGMAN ESL LITERACY offers the most effective way to prepare true beginning adult students for English study.

THE BEGINNING STUDENT

Developed specifically for true beginning adult students, the Second Edition of LONGMAN ESL LITERACY provides a **basic introduction to English** for students who are not ready for Level 1. It assumes that the students using the book may have some literacy skills in their own languages, but not in English. These students may have had little or no prior school experience. LONGMAN ESL LITERACY, Second Edition, offers students who are not ready for the regular ESL Book 1 material the opportunity to learn the basic skills at a gradual, pedagogically sound pace. It prepares students to enter and be successful in a regular ESL Level 1 course. Because the content in LONGMAN ESL LITERACY, Second Edition, parallels most ESL Level 1 courses, the text can also be used in a regular Level 1 class as a supplement for those students requiring additional instruction. Upon completion of the text, the adult student will have the **fundamental literacy skills** needed to succeed academically and the **practical communicative skills** needed to competently function in Level 1.

THE SECOND EDITION OF THE STUDENT BOOK

The STUDENT BOOK has ten units that are topically organized. Every unit also provides students with **life skill competencies** such as filling out forms, reading and writing checks, responding to telephone inquiries and taking messages, and calling for assistance and describing emergencies.

A unique feature of LONGMAN ESL LITERACY has always been the immediate **integration of the basic language skills: listening, speaking, reading, and writing.** The students begin Unit 1, for example, by listening to, repeating, and then writing the letters of the alphabet. Throughout the unit students are given opportunities to *use* the alphabet. They learn to spell their names orally, write their names and those of their classmates, engage in role-plays by asking classmates to spell their names, and write their own names on forms. Language is always presented naturally in realistic contexts. Students learn quickly to read and follow directions, thus becoming actively involved in their own literacy training. The Second Edition of LONGMAN ESL LITERACY builds on this strength by expanding these opportunities for oral interaction. Students not only use new language to learn about their classmates; they use it to talk about them and themselves as well.

Each page in the Second Edition of the STUDENT BOOK is a lesson that is clear and easy to use and teachers can immediately see the communicative purpose of each activity. There are a variety of exercise types included throughout each unit. The exercises were developed to address the **different learning styles of students**. *Teacher's Notes* in the TEACHER'S RESOURCE BOOK suggest specific procedures for presenting the exercises.

KEY EXERCISES

LONGMAN ESL LITERACY, Second Edition, offers a **rich variety of opportunities for literacy practice**. Students circle and write letters and words, listen and write letters, read and write words, read and write sentences, fill out forms, match pictures and words, and match words and sentences. The expanded TEACHER'S RESOURCE BOOK also offers reproducible pages for further practice.

In addition, several key exercises appear regularly throughout LONGMAN ESL LITERACY, Second Edition. Detailed procedures for these key exercises appear in the TEACHER'S RESOURCE BOOK. In the student book, a Teacher's Resource Book icon refers you to that book for reproducible material or a listening script.

SAY THE CONVERSATION.
In this activity, students are provided an important life skill model and are given practice in understanding and responding to **natural conversational English**. Students listen to the teacher model the conversation, and then read and role-play the exchange. Should the teacher also want students to write the conversations, there is literacy line paper at the back of the STUDENT BOOK and reproducible literacy line paper at the back of the TEACHER'S RESOURCE BOOK.

 LISTEN. WATCH THE TEACHER.
This is a **total physical response activity**. Commands with corresponding actions are modeled by the teacher and then performed by the students. Students become physically involved in the lesson. The language presented in *LISTEN. WATCH THE TEACHER* is related to the vocabulary and expressions of the unit.

LISTEN TO THE STORY.
This is a story presented through pictures. Students first listen to the teacher read the story aloud while they look at the pictures in their books. In the Second Edition of LONGMAN ESL LITERACY, students can then **read** the story, which appears with words and pictures on a reproducible page in the TEACHER'S RESOURCE BOOK. Or the teacher can write the story on the chalkboard. Students are then encouraged to **write** the sentences of the story in the correct sequence.

ASK YOUR CLASSMATES.
This student-centered interactive task is based on the previous *SAY THE CONVERSATION* in which students perform personal communicative exchanges. *ASK YOUR CLASSMATES* encourages students to interact with each other and practice the language on their own.

TALK ABOUT YOUR CLASSMATES.
This new activity in the Second Edition encourages students to talk about the information they have learned about their classmates in *ASK YOUR CLASSMATES*. A simple grammar model is provided so they can succeed in this task.

Phonics lesson.
The phonic lessons focus on the correspondence between sound and symbols. Target letters and sounds are always presented in the context of known vocabulary.

 Language experience.
Students relate their own "stories" while the teacher writes words on the board. *Language experience* gives students insight into the relationship between spoken and written language.

 Group activity.
At the end of almost every unit, students get the opportunity to interact with the whole class or a large group.

METHODOLOGY

ESL literacy instruction should **begin with receptive, low-stress activities;** therefore, each lesson in LONGMAN ESL LITERACY, Second Edition, contains ample opportunity for students to develop their listening comprehension skills. The basic methodology is simple: Students listen to the language and absorb it before they produce it and they speak before they read and write. Based on the premise that beginning language learners learn more efficiently if they are engaged in paired and small-group activities, the Second Edition of LONGMAN ESL LITERACY provides an abundance of activities for pair practice or small-group interaction. Each student's opportunity to speak is maximized, and the teacher is free to circulate and address individual needs.

THE EXPANDED TEACHER'S RESOURCE BOOK

The TEACHER'S RESOURCE BOOK has been expanded to contain the following:
- Expanded table of contents that includes a **scope and sequence** of the course, highlighting basic skills, functions, and structures.
- Step-by-step **instructions for key exercise types**.
- *Teacher's Notes* for each unit that present competency objectives, teaching procedures, and new vocabulary.
- **New** reproducible activities and tests
  Supplements—low-level **literacy practice sheets** that provide extra practice for weaker students in tracing and writing letters.
  —a **mechanics activity** that helps students practice how to begin a sentence with a capital letter and end it with a period.
  Readings—**reading activities** that complement LISTEN TO THE STORY in the student book.
  Tests—**literacy tests** for each unit that help you monitor your students' progress.
- Reproducible **alphabet, number, word, and picture flashcards** that provide situational authenticity and enhance students' long-term retention.

UNIT 1
THE ALPHABET

Listen and repeat.

Aa Bb Cc Dd

Ee Ff Gg Hh Ii

Jj Kk Ll Mm

Nn Oo Pp Qq

Rr Ss Tt Uu Vv

Ww Xx Yy Zz

Listen and circle.

A B C D E F G H I J K (L) M
N O P Q R S T U V W X Y Z

Write.

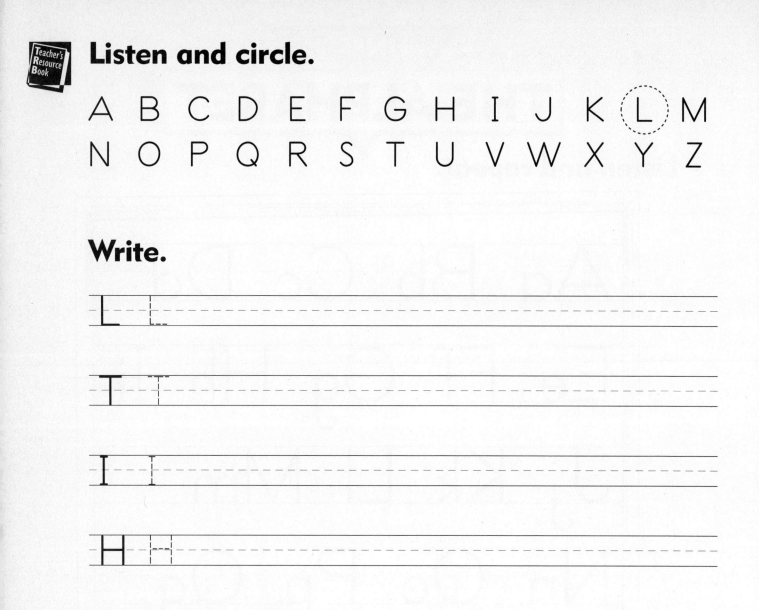

L L

T T

I I

H H

Look and circle.

H	(H)	I	T	H	K	H	E
I	T	Z	I	F	I	H	I
L	I	V	L	T	H	L	L
T	L	T	F	T	I	T	H

Listen and circle.

A B C D E F G H I J K L M
N O P Q R S T U (V) W X Y Z

Write.

V – V

W – W

X – X

Y – Y

Look and circle.

V	(V)	V	Y	V	V	W	N	V	U
W	M	W	V	Z	W	W	X
X	Z	K	X	X	Y	H	X
Y	Y	V	Y	X	W	Y	K

Say the conversation.

A: What's your name?
B: My name is _____.

Write your name.

Listen and circle.

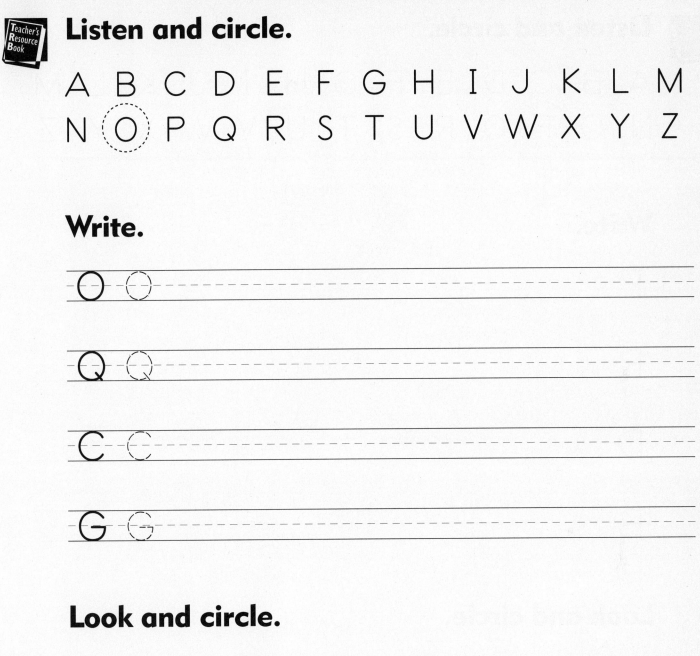

A B C D E F G H I J K L M
N (O) P Q R S T U V W X Y Z

Write.

O O

Q Q

C C

G G

Look and circle.

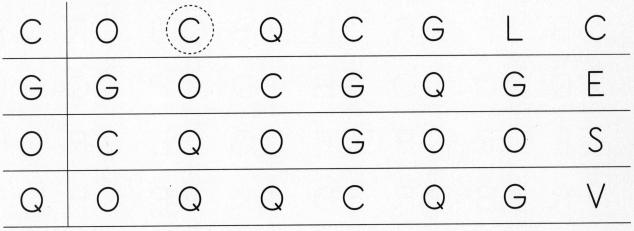

C	O	(C)	Q	C	G	L	C
G	G	O	C	G	Q	G	E
O	C	Q	O	G	O	O	S
Q	O	Q	Q	C	Q	G	V

Listen and circle.

A B C D E F G H I J K L M
N O P Q R S T U V W X Y Z

Write.

P P

R R

D D

B B

Look and circle.

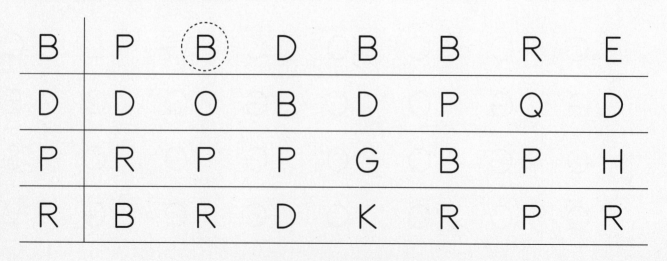

B	P	B	D	B	B	R	E
D	D	O	B	D	P	Q	D
P	R	P	P	G	B	P	H
R	B	R	D	K	R	P	R

Say the conversation.

A: What's your first name?
B: My first name is _____.
A: What's your last name?
B: My last name is _____.

Write.

First Name _____

Last Name _____

Name _____
first   last

Name _____
last   first

Write the capital letters.

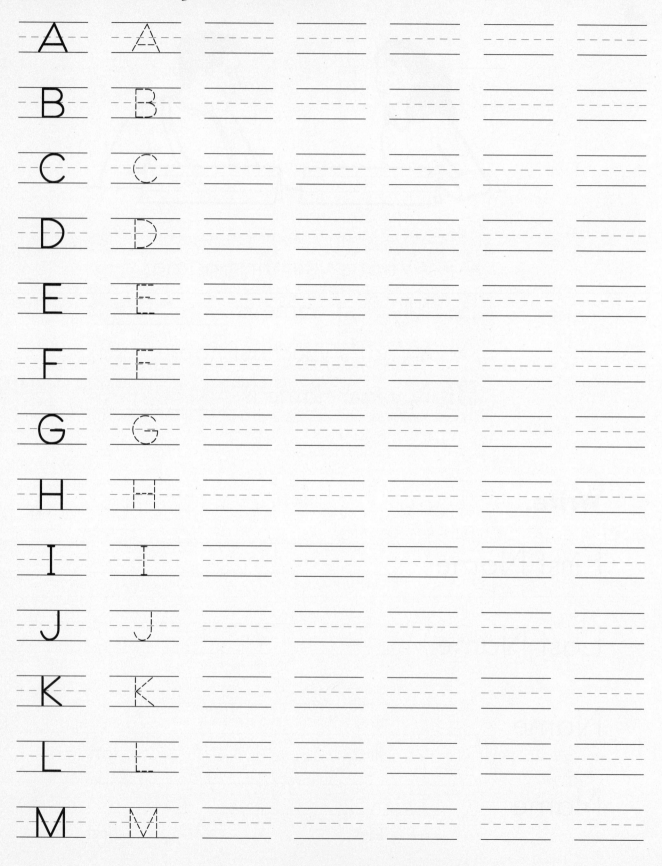

Write the capital letters.

N N

O O

P P

Q Q

R R

S S

T T

U U

V V

W W

X X

Y Y

Z Z

Listen and circle.

a b c d e f g h i j k l m
n o p q (r) s t u v w x y z

Write.

r r

n n

m m

u u

Look and circle.

m	(m)	u	m	n	m	h	r
n	r	n	n	m	v	n	u
r	n	u	r	c	r	m	r
u	u	v	u	n	y	u	r

10

Listen and circle.

a b c d e f g ⓗ i j k l m
n o p q r s t u v w x y z

Write.

h h
b b
t t
f f

Look and circle.

b	ⓑ	d	h	b	l	b	d
f	t	k	f	f	b	l	f
h	h	b	t	h	n	h	d
t	x	t	f	t	l	k	t

Listen.

Write an A.

Say A.

Circle the A.

Now you try.

Look and circle.

1.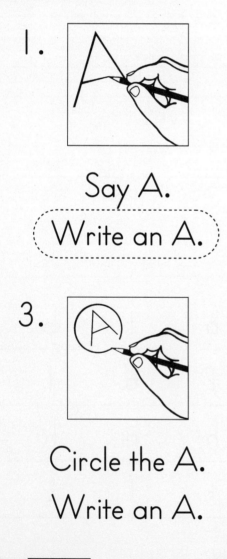

Say A.

(Write an A.)

2.

Listen.

Circle the A.

3.

Circle the A.

Write an A.

4.

Say A.

Listen.

Listen and circle.

a b c d e f g h i j k l m
n (o) p q r s t u v w x y z

Write.

o o

c c

a a

d d

Look and circle.

a	d	(a)	a	o	c	a	b
c	a	o	c	e	c	d	c
d	d	a	d	d	b	o	h
o	b	o	a	p	o	c	o

Listen and circle.

a b c d e f g h i (j) k l m
n o p q r s t u v w x y z

Write.

j j

g g

q q

p p

Look and circle.

g	j	(g)	g	a	q	g	p
j	i	q	j	j	p	g	j
p	p	b	p	q	d	p	g
q	g	q	q	b	j	q	a

Ask your teacher.
Ask a classmate.

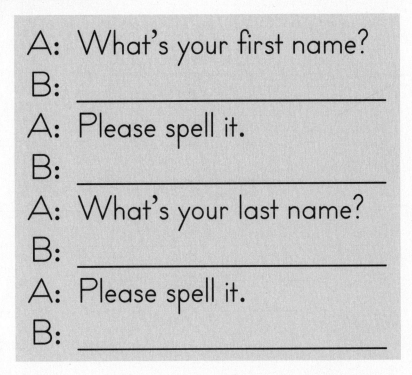

A: What's your first name?
B: _____
A: Please spell it.
B: _____
A: What's your last name?
B: _____
A: Please spell it.
B: _____

Write the first name and last name.

	First Name	Last Name
Teacher		
Classmate		

Talk about your teacher.
Talk about your classmate.

My teacher's first name is _____.

Write the small letters.

a   a

b   b

c   c

d   d

e   e

f   f

g   g

h   h

i   i

j   j

k   k

l   l

m   m

Write the small letters.

n   n

o   o

p   p

q   q

r   r

s   s

t   t

u   u

v   v

w   w

x   x

y   y

z   z

Look and circle.

Name	(Name)	Mane	Name	Mean
First	Four	First	First	Start
Last	Lost	Last	Stall	Last

Write.

Name _____

Name _____ , _____
                last   first

Name _____   _____
                first   last

First Name _____

Last Name _____

Name _____

Say the alphabet.

A a　B b　C c　D d　E e　F f　G g
H h　I i　J j　K k　L l　M m　N n
O o　P p　Q q　R r　S s　T t　U u
V v　W w　X x　Y y　Z z

Write the capital letters.

A ___ ___ ___ E ___ ___

___ I ___ ___ ___ N

___ ___ ___ R ___ ___

V ___ ___ ___ ___ ___

Write the small letters.

___ b ___ ___ ___ ___ ___

___ ___ ___ ___ ___ m ___

___ ___ ___ ___ ___ ___ ___

___ ___ ___ y ___

REVIEW

Listen and circle.

(f)	E	(F)	b	T
P	R	k	h	r
U	v	N	u	x
O	q	D	Q	a
j	y	Y	g	I

Write the capital letters.

w W   i _____   a _____

d _____   s _____   g _____

h _____   y _____   k _____

Write the small letters.

T t _____   W _____   C _____

M _____   R _____   J _____

B _____   N _____   L _____

20

Ask your classmates.

A: What's your first name?

B: _____

A: What's your last name?

B: _____

A: Please spell your name.

B: _____

Write your classmates' names.

First Name	Last Name

Listen and repeat.

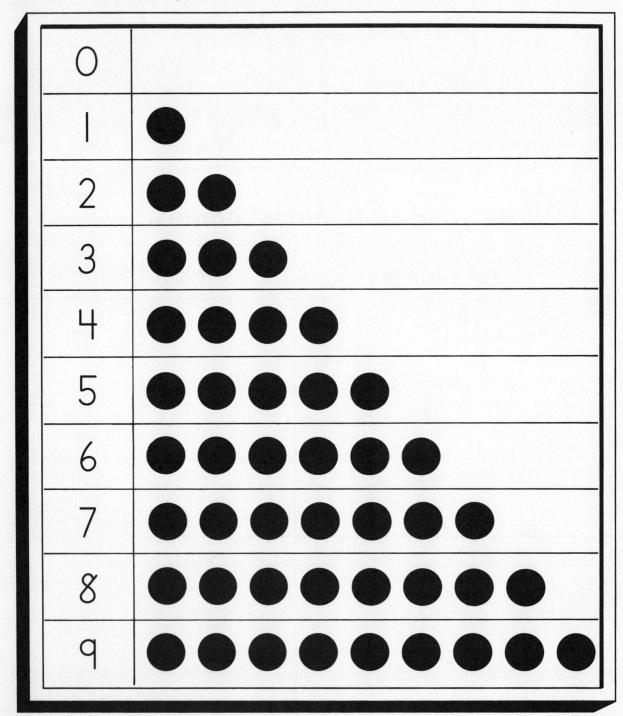

Write the numbers.

Look and circle.

● ● ● ●	5 ⟨4⟩ 3	● ● — 2 1 3
● ● ● ● ● ● ●	6 8 7	● ● ● ● ● — 3 4 5
● ● ●	5 3 4	● ● ● ● ● ● ● ● ● — 8 9 7
● ● ● ● ● ●	6 8 9	● — 0 1 7
● ● ● ●	2 4 6	● ● ● ● ● ● ● ● ● — 8 6 9
● ● ● ● ● ● ● ●	8 2 7	● ● ● — 4 3 2

24

Write your telephone number.

(_____) _____ — _____

area code

(_____) _____ — _____

(_____) _____ — _____

 Say the conversation.

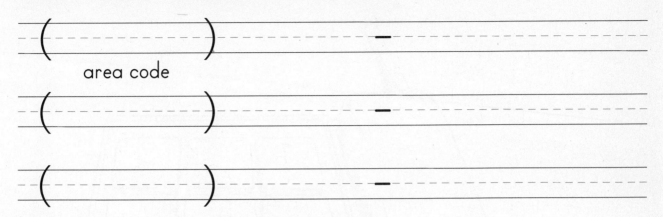

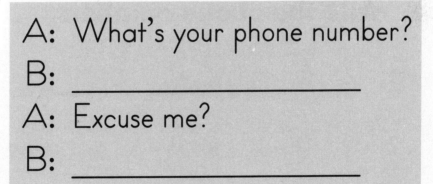

A: What's your phone number?

B: _____

A: Excuse me?

B: _____

 **Now ask your classmate. Write the telephone number.**

(_____) _____ — _____

Write the numbers.

Listen. Write the phone numbers.

1. 6 2 6 – 7 1 5 3

2. 3 _ 9 – 8 4 _ _

3. 5 _ _ – 0 _ _ 7

4. _ 1 _ – _ _ _ 9

Write your address.

_____

number   street

_____

number   street

_____

number   street

Say the conversation.

Main Street

number   street

A: What's your address?
B: My address is _____.
A: Excuse me?
B: _____

Now ask your classmate. Write the address.

_____

number   street

Say the conversation.

A: Hello.
B: Hello.
A: How are you?
B: Fine, thank you.

Write the answers.

1. How are you?

   Fine, thank you.

2. What's your name?

3. What's your address?

4. What's your phone number?

   (   )   —

Now ask a classmate.

Listen. Watch the teacher.

Stand up.
Smile.
Shake hands.
Sit down.

Now you try.

Look and circle.

1.

   (Smile.)
   Stand up.

2.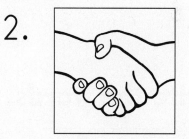

   Sit down.
   Shake hands.

3.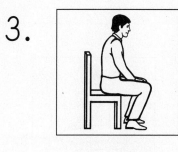

   Smile.
   Sit down.

4.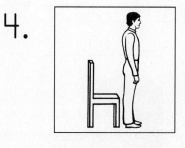

   Stand up.
   Shake hands.

Write the capital S and small s.

S

s

Listen. Write s.

__s__ ay

__ it

__ tand

__ mile

Write the words.

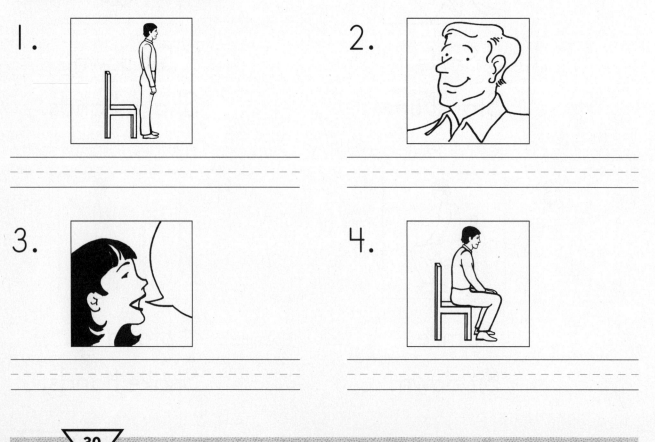

1.

2.

3.

4.

Say the words.

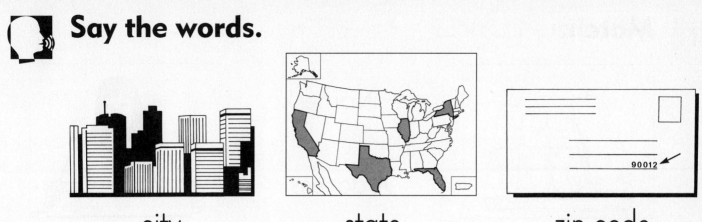

city   state   zip code

Say your city and state.

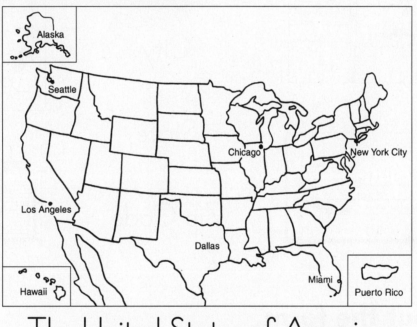

The United States of America

Write.

1. Write your city.

2. Write your state.

3. Write your zip code.

Match.

Name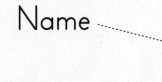

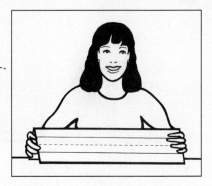

Address

Telephone

City

State

Zip Code

Fill out the form.

Name _____

           first   last

Address _____

City _____ State _____

Zip Code _____ Telephone (___) _____

Ask your classmates.

A: What's your address?

B: _____

A: Please write it.

B: OK. Here you are.

A: Thank you.

Write the addresses.

	Address
Classmate 1	
Classmate 2	
Classmate 3	
Classmate 4	

Talk about your classmates.

Mario**'s address is** _____.

Write to your teacher.

_____

name

_____

address

_____

city   state   zip code

STAMP

_____

name

_____

address

_____

city   state   zip code

Write to a classmate.

_____

_____

_____

_____

Listen to the story.

1.

2.

3.

4.

Read the story.

Write the story.

1. _____

2. _____

3. _____

4. _____

Check the answer.

1. Do you go to school?

☑ Yes, I do.

☐ No, I don't.

2. Do you go to work?

☐ Yes, I do.

☐ No, I don't.

3. Do you study English?

☐ Yes, I do.

☐ No, I don't.

4. Do you walk home?

☐ Yes, I do.

☐ No, I don't.

 **Now ask a classmate.**

Write the capital N and small n.

N

n

Listen. Write n.

<u>n</u>ame ___o

__umber dow__

Write the words.

1. What's your phone ———————?

2. Yes / No ———————, I don't.

3. Please sit ———————.

4. What's your ———————?

Circle the word.

1. name   m a n a m e n e
2. phone   e p h o n e h o n p h
3. address   d e s a d d r e s s e
4. city   c i t c i t y c y t i y
5. state   e s t a t a t s t a t e
6. zip code   p z i p d o z c o d e d

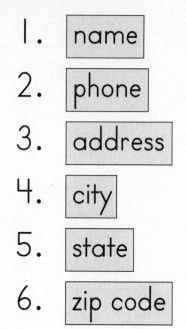

Separate the words.

1. What'syourname?

   What's your name?

2. What'syouraddress?

3. What'syourzipcode?

4. What'syourphonenumber?

Fill out the form.

Name _____ , _____
        last   first

Address _____
          number   street

        _____
          city   state   zip code

Phone number (_____) _____

 ## Ask your classmates.

A: What's your area code?

B: _____

A: What's your phone number?

B: _____

Write the numbers.

	Area Code	Phone Number
Classmate 1		
Classmate 2		
Classmate 3		

 ## Talk about your classmates.

Carla's phone number is _____ .

Listen.

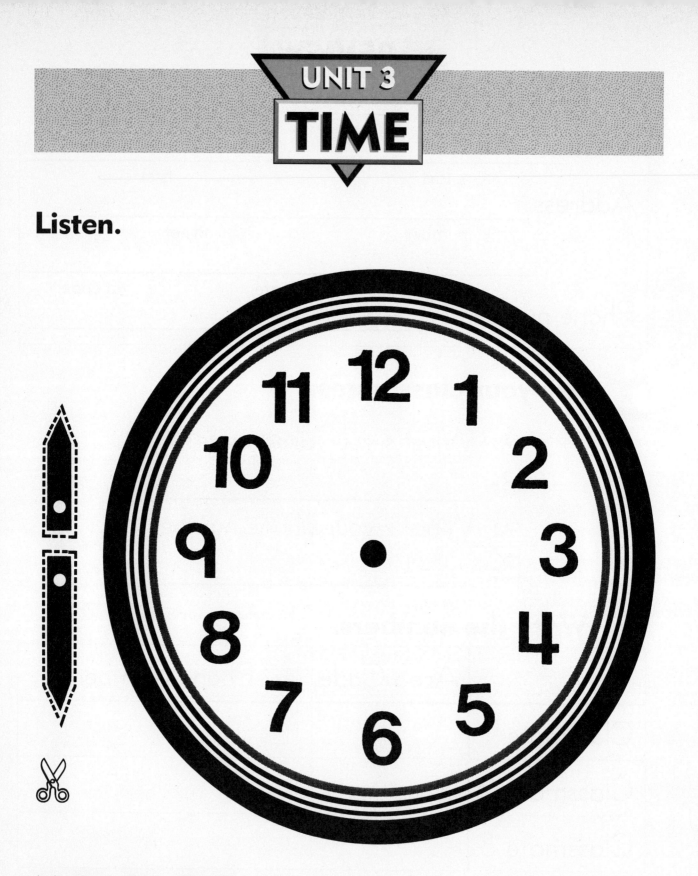

Make the clock.

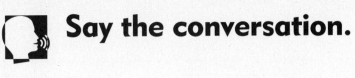

A: What time is it?
B: It's <u>6:00</u>.
A: Thank you.
B: You're welcome.

Use the clock on page 40.
Say the time.

1. 6:00
2. 3:00
3. 9:00
4. 1:00
5. 11:00

6. 12:00
7. 8:00
8. 4:00
9. 10:00
10. 7:00

Write T and t.

T _ _ _ _ _ _ _ _ _

t _ _ _ _ _ _ _ _ _

Listen. Write t.

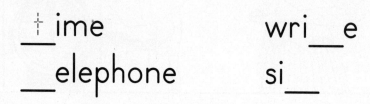

_t_ ime   wri __ e

__ elephone   si __

Write the words.

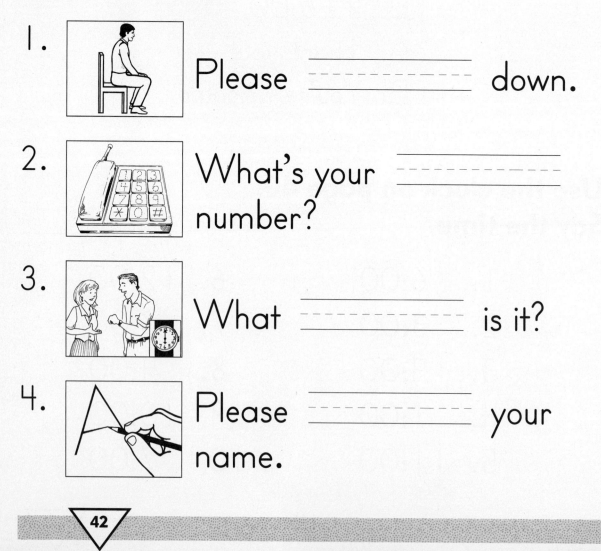

1. Please _ _ _ _ _ down.

2. What's your _ _ _ _ _ number?

3. What _ _ _ _ _ is it?

4. Please _ _ _ _ _ your name.

Listen and repeat. Write the numbers.

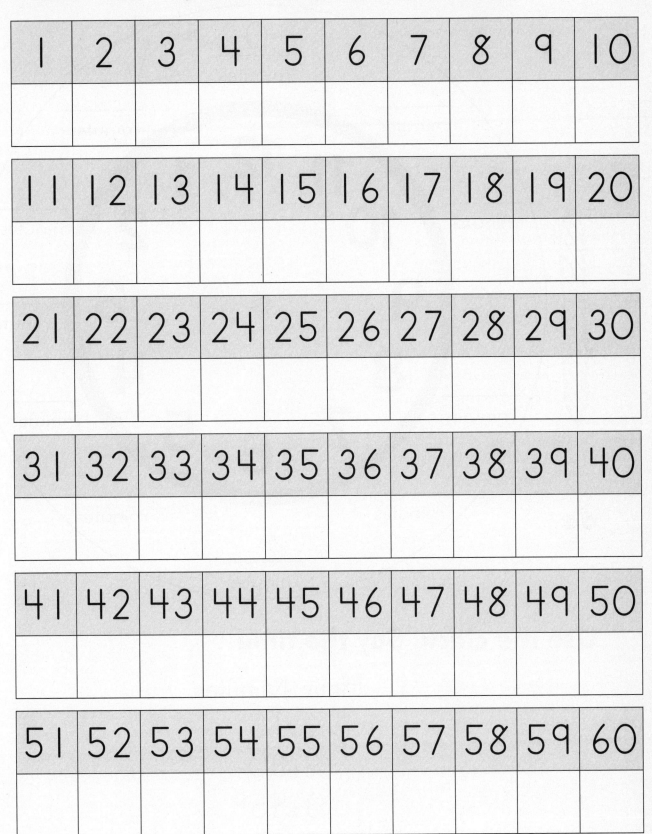

1	2	3	4	5	6	7	8	9	10

11	12	13	14	15	16	17	18	19	20

21	22	23	24	25	26	27	28	29	30

31	32	33	34	35	36	37	38	39	40

41	42	43	44	45	46	47	48	49	50

51	52	53	54	55	56	57	58	59	60

Write the minutes.

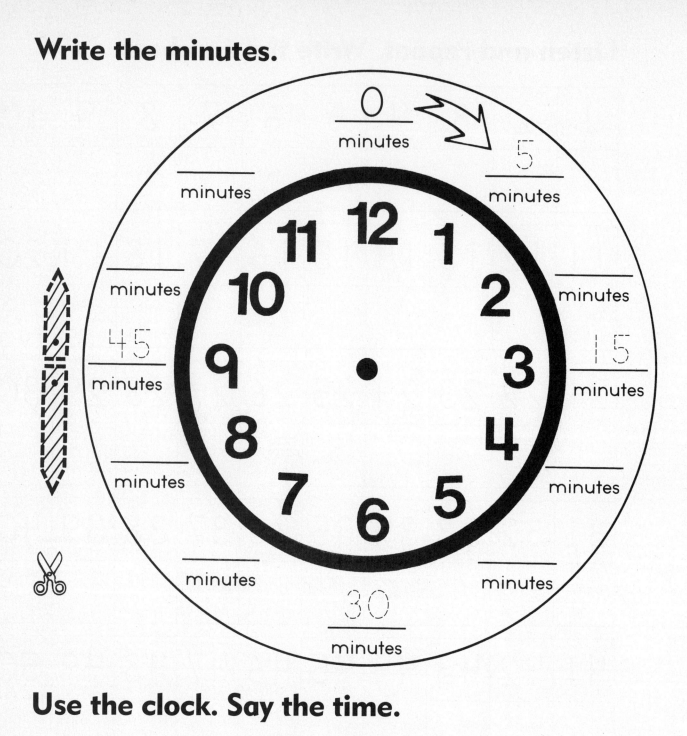

0 minutes

5 minutes

minutes

minutes

45 minutes

15 minutes

minutes

minutes

minutes

minutes

30 minutes

Use the clock. Say the time.

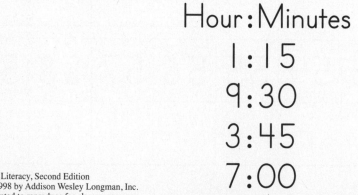

Hour : Minutes

1 : 15

9 : 30

3 : 45

7 : 00

Say and write the time.

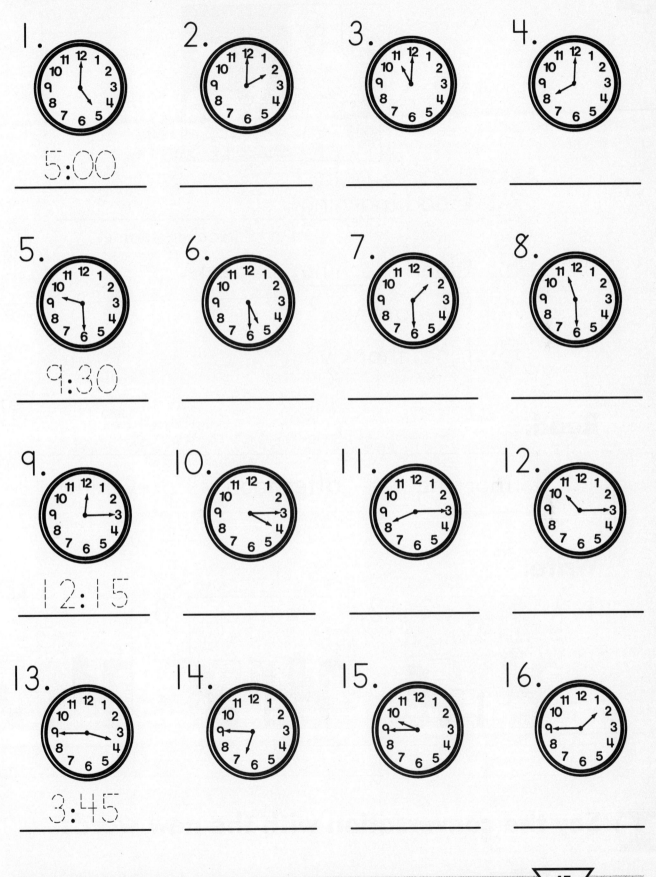

1. 5:00

2. _____

3. _____

4. _____

5. 9:30

6. _____

7. _____

8. _____

9. 12:15

10. _____

11. _____

12. _____

13. 3:45

14. _____

15. _____

16. _____

Say the conversation.

A: Good <u>morning</u>, _____.

teacher's name

B: Good <u>morning</u>, students.

A: How are you?

B: Fine, thank you.

Read.

| morning | afternoon | evening |

Write.

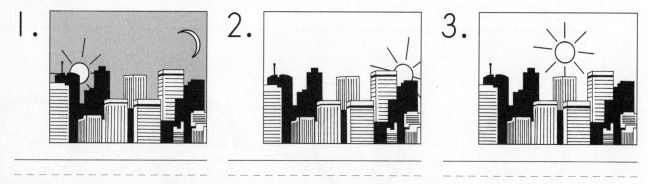

1. _____

2. _____

3. _____

 **Say the conversation with the new words.**

Say the numbers.

1	2	3	4	5	6	7	8	9	10
11	12	13	14	15	16	17	18	19	20
21	22	23	24	25	26	27	28	29	30
31	32	33	34	35	36	37	38	39	40
41	42	43	44	45	46	47	48	49	50
51	52	53	54	55	56	57	58	59	60
61	62	63	64	65	66	67	68	69	70
71	72	73	74	75	76	77	78	79	80
81	82	83	84	85	86	87	88	89	90
91	92	93	94	95	96	97	98	99	100

Write the numbers.

1				5					
		13							20
						27			
	32								
								49	
			54						
61									
						76			
								88	
									100

Listen and repeat. Circle teen. Write.

13 thir(teen)   ~~thirteen~~ _____

14 fourteen   _____

15 fifteen   _____

16 sixteen   _____

17 seventeen   _____

18 eighteen   _____

19 nineteen   _____

Listen and repeat. Circle ty. Write.

20 twen(ty)   ~~twenty~~ _____

30 thirty   _____

40 forty   _____

50 fifty   _____

60 sixty   _____

70 seventy   _____

80 eighty   _____

90 ninety   _____

Say the conversation.

A: Goodbye, _____.
 teacher's name

B: Goodbye, students.

A: See you tomorrow.

B: See you tomorrow. Please come
   on time at _____.
                    time

Draw the time. Say the time.

1.

10:15

2.

4:00

3.

7:45

4.

1:30

5.

9:45

6.

12:15

TPR **Listen. Watch the teacher.**

Look at your watch.

Look at the clock.

Say the time.

Write the time.

Now you try.

Look and circle.

1.

Look at the clock.

Look at your watch.

2.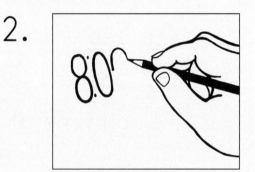

Say the time.

Write the time.

3.

Say the time.

Look at the clock.

4.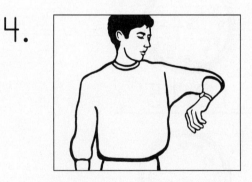

Write the time.

Look at your watch.

Listen to the story.

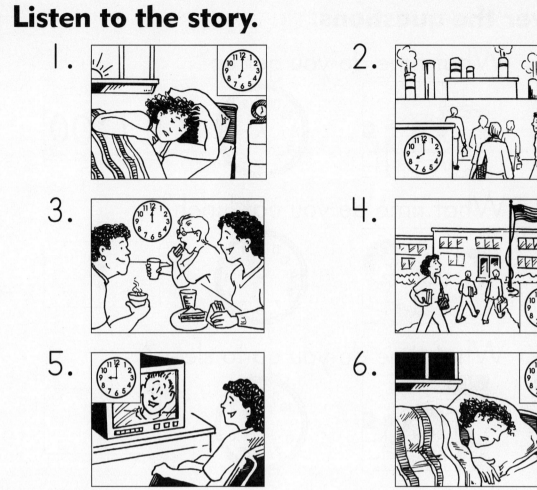

1.

2.

3.

4.

5.

6.

Read the story.

Write the story.

1. _____

2. _____

3. _____

4. _____

5. _____

6. _____

Answer the questions.

1. What time do you get up?

7:00

2. What time do you eat lunch?

:

3. What time do you go to sleep?

:

Now ask your classmates. Write the time.

	Get Up	Eat Lunch	Go to Sleep
Classmate 1			
Classmate 2			
Classmate 3			

Talk about your classmates.

I **get** up at 7:00.   Kim **gets** up at 8:00.

Say the conversation.

A: When is the <u>bank</u> open?
B: From <u>10</u> to <u>3</u>.
A: Excuse me. What time?
B: It opens at <u>10:00</u>.
   It closes at <u>3:00</u>.

Read.

restaurant   post office   market

Write.

1. _____
   - - - - - - - - - -
   _____

2. _____
   - - - - - - - - - -
   _____

3. _____
   - - - - - - - - - -
   _____

Say the conversation with the new words.

Write G and g.

G _____

g _____

Read.

go

get up

goodbye

Write the words.

1. I _____ _____ at 7:00.

2. I _____ to school.

3. _____. See you tomorrow.

Listen. Write t or g.

1. __omorrow

2. __et

3. __ood

4. __ime

5. marke__

6. __oodbye

7. __o

8. ge__

Answer the questions.

1. When do you eat lunch?
   From ___12:00___ to ___12:30___.
2. When do you work?
   From _____ to _____.

Fill out the form.

Name _____
        first   last
Address _____

_____ _____ _____
        city   state   zip code
Telephone (_____) _____

	From	To
Work		
Eat Lunch		
Study English		
Watch TV		
Sleep		

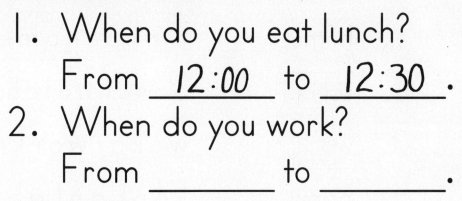

Ask your classmates questions.

When do you _____ ?

Circle the word.

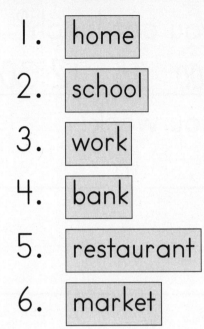

1. home   o m h o e h o m e o
2. school   o o s c h o o l c h
3. work   w o k o r w o r k r
4. bank   k a n b a n k a b n
5. restaurant   r a n t r e s t a u r a n t
6. market   m a r k e t m a k e t

Separate the words.

1. Whattimeisit?

What time is it?

2. Whattimedoyougotoschool?

3. Whattimedoyougotowork?

4. Whattimedoyougohome?

Match.

1. I get up
2. I go to sleep
3. I watch TV
4. I work
5. I study English
6. I go to the bank

 in the morning.

 in the afternoon.

 in the evening.

Ask your classmates.

A: When do you go to the <u>bank</u>?
B: In the _____ .

Write morning, afternoon, **or** evening.

	Bank	Market	Post Office
Classmate 1			
Classmate 2			
Classmate 3			

 Talk about your classmates.

I go to the bank in the morning.
Ming goes to the bank in the afternoon.

Listen.

SUNDAY	MONDAY	TUESDAY	WEDNESDAY	THURSDAY	FRIDAY	SATURDAY
1	2	3	4	5	6	7
8	9	10	11	12	13	14
15	16	17	18	19	20	21
22	23	24	25	26	27	28
29	30	31				

Match.

Sunday   Tues.

Monday   Mon.

Tuesday   Wed.

Wednesday   Sun.

Thursday   Sat.

Friday   Thurs.

Saturday   Fri.

Write the words.

1. Fri.   Friday

2. Mon.   _____

3. Thurs.   _____

4. Sun.   _____

5. Tues.   _____

6. Sat.   _____

7. Wed.   _____

Say the conversation.

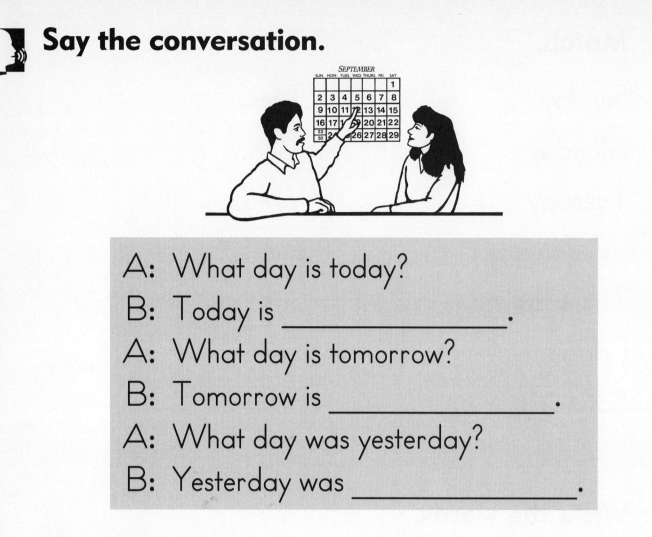

A: What day is today?

B: Today is _____.

A: What day is tomorrow?

B: Tomorrow is _____.

A: What day was yesterday?

B: Yesterday was _____.

Write the days.

	Yesterday	Today	Tomorrow
1.	Monday	Tuesday	
2.	Saturday		Monday
3.		Friday	
4.			Thursday

Make a calendar for this month.

_____
month

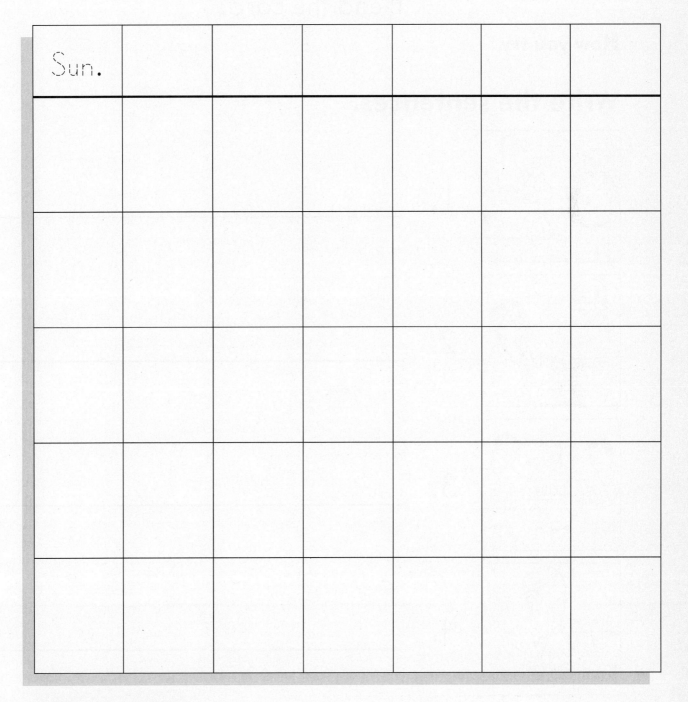

Sun.						

Listen. Watch the teacher.

Come here.
Take a card.
Line up.
Read the card.

Now you try.

Write the sentences.

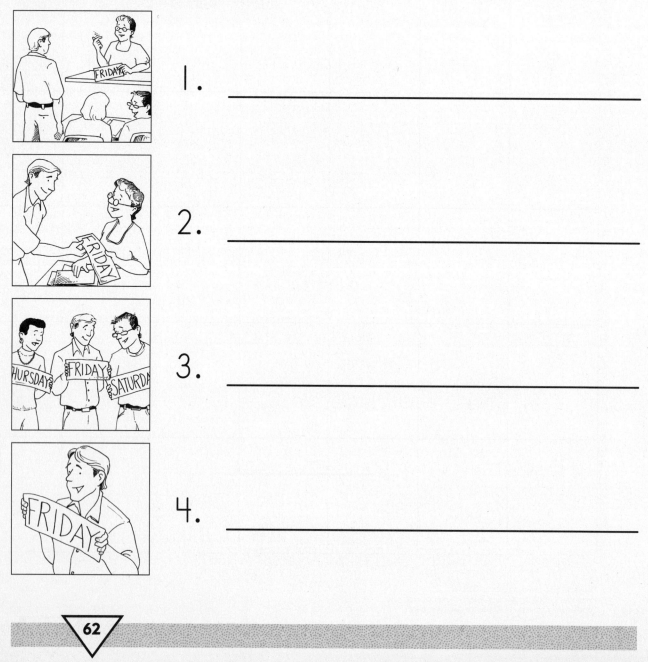

1. _____

2. _____

3. _____

4. _____

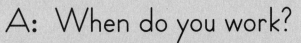 **Ask your classmates.**

> A: When do you work?
> B: Monday to Friday.
> A: Do you work on Sunday?
> B: _____
> A: Do you work on Thursday?
> B: _____

Write yes **or** no.

	Sun.	Mon.	Tues.	Wed.	Thurs.	Fri.	Sat.
Classmate 1							
Classmate 2							
Classmate 3							
Classmate 4							

Talk about your classmates.

> I **work** on Saturday and Sunday.
> Ahmed **works** Monday to Friday.

Write D **and** d.

D — — — — — — — — —

d — — — — — — — — —

Read the words. Circle day.

today	Monday	Thursday
yesterday	Tuesday	Friday
Sunday	Wednesday	

Listen. Write D **or** d.

A: __o you stu__y English?

B: Yes, I __o.

A: __o you go to school on Sun__ay?

B: No, I __on't.

Now say the conversation with a classmate.

Read the months.

January	July
February	August
March	September
April	October
May	November
June	December

Write the months.

1. June _June_
2. Oct. _October_
3. Mar. _____
4. July _____
5. Apr. _____
6. Dec. _____

7. Aug. _____
8. Jan. _____
9. May _____
10. Nov. _____
11. Feb. _____
12. Sept. _____

 Choose a month.
Tell your classmates the month.
Line up in order.

Say the conversation.

SEPTEMBER

SUN.	MON.	TUES.	WED.	THURS.	FRI.	SAT.
						1
2	3	4	5	6	7	8
9	10	11	12	13	14	15
16	17	18	19	20	21	22
23 30	24	25	26	27	28	29

A: What day is today?

B: Today is _____.

A: What's the month?

B: The month is _____.

A: What's the year?

B: The year is _____.

Write the date.

1. Today is _____ _____, _____.
   month   day   year

2. Tomorrow is _____ _____, _____.
   month   day   year

3. Yesterday was _____ _____, _____.
   month   day   year

Say the conversation.

A: When were you born?

B: _____ _____, _____
       month   day   year

Write your date of birth.

Date of Birth _____ _____, _____
(DOB)   month   day   year

Birthdate _____ _____, _____
        month   day   year

Write your birthdate with numbers.

Date of Birth ____ – ____ – ____
(DOB)   month   day   year

Birthdate ____ – ____ – ____
    month   day   year

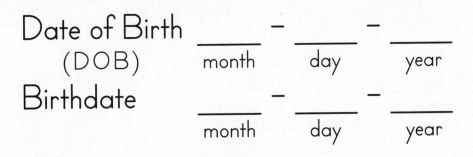 **Ask your classmates:** When were you born?
Line up in order.

Say the conversation.

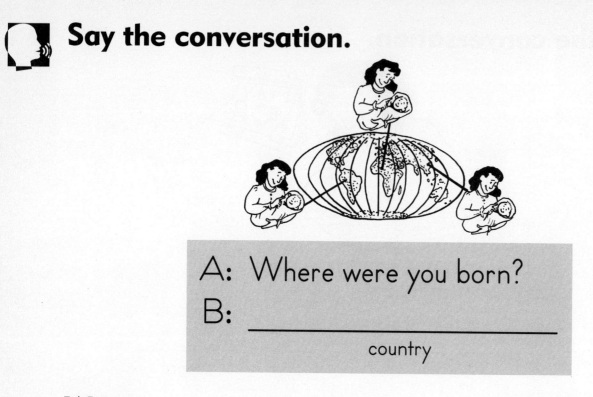

A: Where were you born?

B: _____
                    country

Write.

Place of Birth _____

Birthplace _____

Fill out the form.

Date _____

Last Name _____ First Name _____

Address _____

City _____ State _____ Zip Code _____

Telephone (_____) _____

Birthdate _____

Birthplace _____

Write Y and y.

Y ------- ------- ------- ------- ------- ------- ------- -------

y ------- ------- ------- ------- ------- ------- ------- -------

Read. Circle the words beginning with y.

A: Was yesterday your birthday?
B: Yes, it was.
A: How old are you?
B: I'm 30 years old.
A: Happy Birthday!

Write the words with y.

1. y _____

2. y _____

3. y _____

4. y _____

5. y _____

Listen to the story.

1.  **Sun.**

2.  **Mon.** Ms.Lav.

3. **Tues.**  **Thurs.**

4.  **Wed.**

5. **Fri.**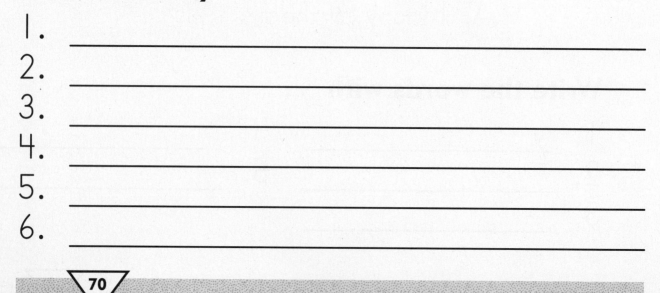

6. **Sat.**

Read the story.

Write the story.

1. _____
2. _____
3. _____
4. _____
5. _____
6. _____

Answer the questions.

1.  When do you go shopping?

   I go shopping on _____.
   day

2.  When do you clean the house?

   I clean the house on _____.

3.  When do you eat at a restaurant?

   I eat at a restaurant on _____.

4.  When do you do the laundry?

   I do the _____ on _____.

5.  When do you study English?

   I _____ English on _____.

6. 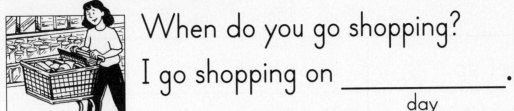 When do you go to the bank?

   I ____ to the _____ on _____.

Now ask a classmate.

Write the time.

	Sun.	Mon.	Tues.	Wed.	Thurs.	Fri.	Sat.
I get up.							
I go to work.							
I eat lunch.							
I go to school.							
I watch TV.							
I go to sleep.							

Ask a classmate. Write the time.

1. What time do you get up on Sunday? _____

2. What time do you go to work on Monday? _____

3. What time do you eat lunch on Tuesday? _____

4. What time do you go to sleep on Friday? _____

5. What time do you watch TV on Saturday? _____

Talk about your classmate.

I **eat** lunch at 12:00 on Tuesday.
Mario **eats** lunch at 12:30 on Tuesday.

Separate the words.

1. DoyougotoschoolonTuesday?

   <u>Do you</u>

2. DoyougotoworkonTuesday?

   _____

3. DoyougoshoppingonTuesday?

   _____

 Now ask your classmates. Write yes **or** no.

	Tuesday		
	School	Work	Shopping
Classmate 1			
Classmate 2			
Classmate 3			
Classmate 4			

 Talk about your classmates.

Lee **goes** to work on Tuesday.
Linda **doesn't go** to work on Tuesday.

Ask your classmates.

What month is your birthday?

Write the names in the birthday calendar.

January	February	March
_____	_____	_____
_____	_____	_____
_____	_____	_____
April	**May**	**June**
_____	_____	_____
_____	_____	_____
_____	_____	_____
_____	_____	_____
July	**August**	**September**
_____	_____	_____
_____	_____	_____
_____	_____	_____
October	**November**	**December**
_____	_____	_____
_____	_____	_____
_____	_____	_____

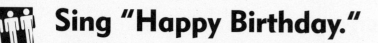 **Sing "Happy Birthday."**

Teacher's Resource Book

Listen.

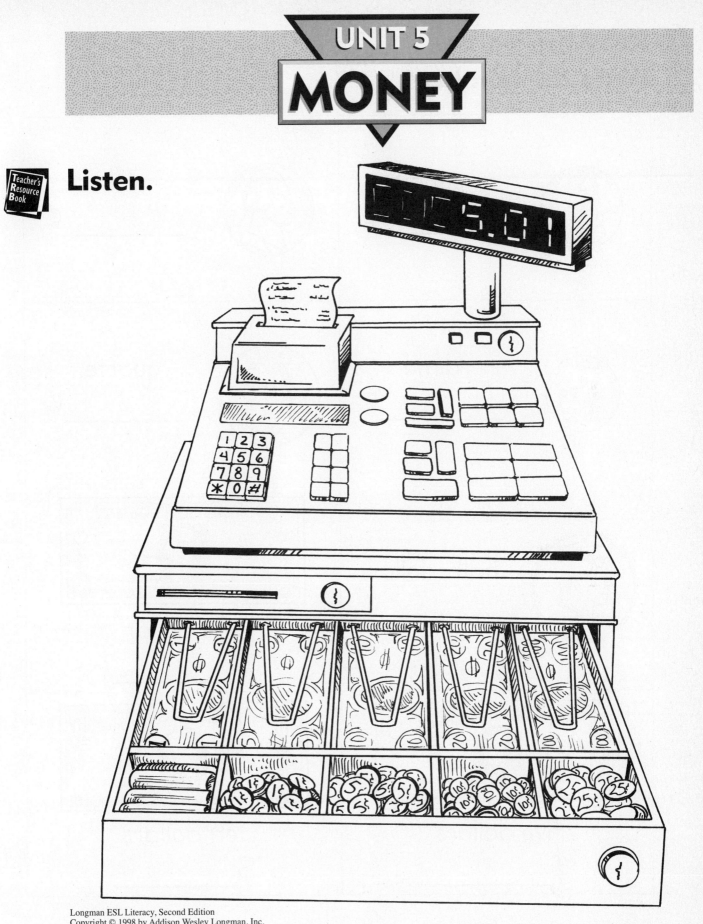

Read the words.
Write the numbers.

penny

___1___ ¢

nickel

___5___ ¢

dime

_____ ¢

quarter

_____ ¢

half-dollar

_____ ¢

one dollar

$ ___1.00___

five dollars

$ _____

ten dollars

$ _____

Add the money.

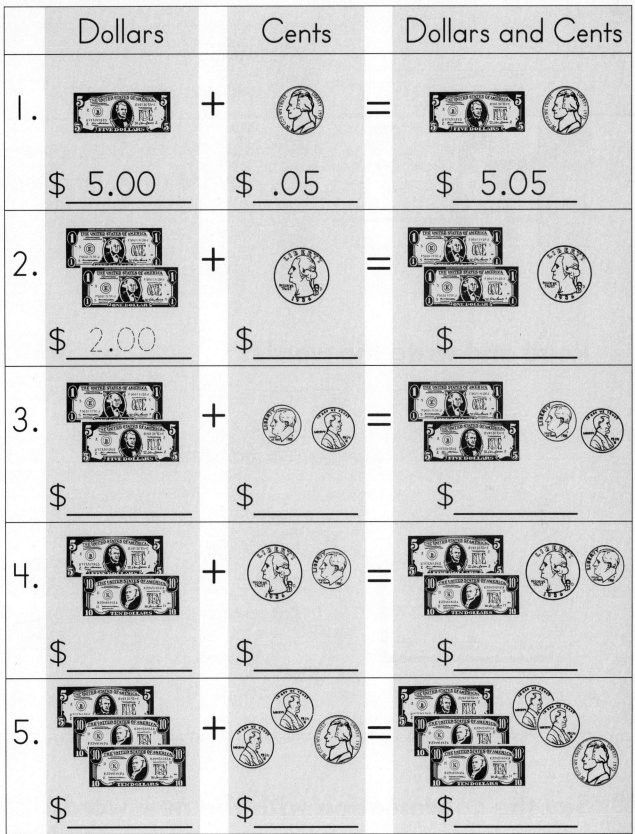

	Dollars		Cents		Dollars and Cents
1.	$ 5.00	+	$ .05	=	$ 5.05
2.	$ 2.00	+	$ _____	=	$ _____
3.	$ _____	+	$ _____	=	$ _____
4.	$ _____	+	$ _____	=	$ _____
5.	$ _____	+	$ _____	=	$ _____

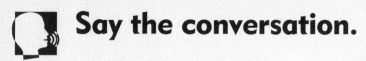

Say the conversation.

ABC Store

A: May I help you?
B: How much is this?
A: It's $14.00.
B: I want to buy it, please.
A: Cash or charge?
B: <u>Cash</u>.

Read and write the words.

| cash | charge | check |

1.

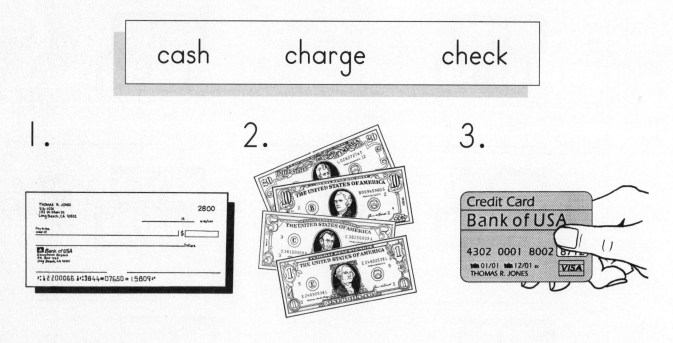

THOMAS R. JONES
105 W. Main St.
Long Beach, CA 90802

2800

2.

3.

Credit Card
Bank of USA
4302 0001 8002 8712
01/01 12/01
THOMAS R. JONES
VISA

_____

_____

_____

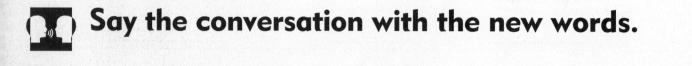

Say the conversation with the new words.

1.	$.05	$.10	$.15
2.	$.25	$.50	$.75
3.	$.40	$.60	$.80
4.	$.55	$.65	$.95

5.	$10	$20	$30
6.	$11	$12	$13
7.	$15	$50	$55
8.	$78	$87	$88

9.	$12.50	$22.50	$32.50
10.	$28.10	$58.20	$88.30
11.	$9.50	$5.90	$9.05
12.	$17.85	$85.17	$70.80

Say the words. Write the numbers.

1	One
2	Two
___	Three
___	Four
___	Five
___	Six
___	Seven
___	Eight
___	Nine
10	Ten
___	Eleven
___	Twelve
13	Thirteen
___	Fourteen
___	Fifteen
___	Sixteen
___	Seventeen
___	Eighteen
19	Nineteen
___	Twenty
___	Twenty-one
22	Twenty-two
___	Twenty-three
___	Twenty-four
___	Twenty-five

___	Twenty-six
___	Twenty-seven
___	Twenty-eight
29	Twenty-nine
___	Thirty
___	Thirty-one
___	Thirty-two
33	Thirty-three
___	Thirty-four
___	Thirty-five
36	Thirty-six
___	Thirty-seven
___	Thirty-eight
___	Thirty-nine
___	Forty
___	Forty-one
42	Forty-two
___	Forty-three
___	Forty-four
___	Forty-five
___	Forty-six
___	Forty-seven
___	Forty-eight
___	Forty-nine
50	Fifty

Read the check.

PAY TO _ABC Market_ $ _14.00_

March 8, 1998

Fourteen and no/100 ~~~~~ DOLLARS

Mary Lee

Write the check for $38.00.

_____

PAY TO _____ $ _____

_____ DOLLARS

_____

Write the check for $50.00.

_____

PAY TO _____ $ _____

_____ DOLLARS

_____

Say the words. Write the numbers.

51	Fifty-one	_____	Seventy-six
_____	Fifty-two	_____	Seventy-seven
_____	Fifty-three	_____	Seventy-eight
_____	Fifty-four	_____	Seventy-nine
55	Fifty-five	80	Eighty
_____	Fifty-six	_____	Eighty-one
_____	Fifty-seven	_____	Eighty-two
58	Fifty-eight	83	Eighty-three
_____	Fifty-nine	_____	Eighty-four
_____	Sixty	_____	Eighty-five
61	Sixty-one	_____	Eighty-six
_____	Sixty-two	_____	Eighty-seven
_____	Sixty-three	_____	Eighty-eight
_____	Sixty-four	89	Eighty-nine
_____	Sixty-five	_____	Ninety
_____	Sixty-six	_____	Ninety-one
_____	Sixty-seven	92	Ninety-two
_____	Sixty-eight	_____	Ninety-three
69	Sixty-nine	_____	Ninety-four
_____	Seventy	_____	Ninety-five
_____	Seventy-one	_____	Ninety-six
72	Seventy-two	_____	Ninety-seven
_____	Seventy-three	_____	Ninety-eight
_____	Seventy-four	_____	Ninety-nine
_____	Seventy-five	100	One hundred

Write the words.

1. 14 _____
2. 38 _____
3. 72 _____
4. 99 _____
5. 65 _____

Write the numbers.

1. Thirty-three _____
2. Nineteen _____
3. Eighty-one _____
4. Fifty-six _____
5. Twenty-five _____
6. Ninety-two _____
7. Forty-four _____
8. One hundred _____
9. Eleven _____
10. Sixty _____

Read the check.

April 27, 1998

PAY TO _ABC Market_ $ _87.50_

Eighty-seven and 50/100 ~~~~~~~~ DOLLARS

Mary Lee

Write the check for $61.99.

_____

PAY TO _____ $ _____

_____ DOLLARS

_____

Write the check for $90.18.

_____

PAY TO _____ $ _____

_____ DOLLARS

_____

A: Do you have change?

B: Yes, I do.

A: Do you have <u>quarters</u>?

B: No, I don't.

A: Do you have <u>dimes</u>?

B: Yes, I do. I have <u>five dimes</u>.

Now say the conversation with new words.

Match.

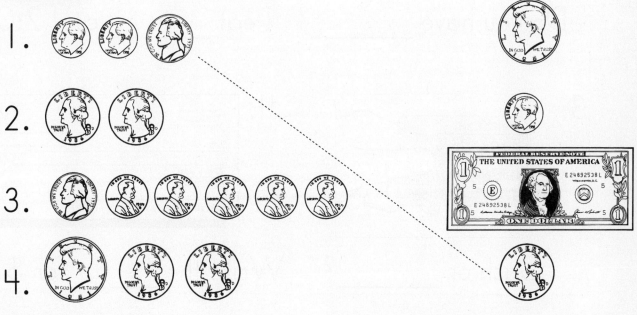

1.

2.

3.

4.

Write Ch **and** ch.

Ch ‗ ‗ ‗ ‗ ‗ ‗ ‗ ‗

ch ‗ ‗ ‗ ‗ ‗ ‗ ‗ ‗

Listen. Write ch.

___eck   ___ange

___arge   lun___

Write the words.

1.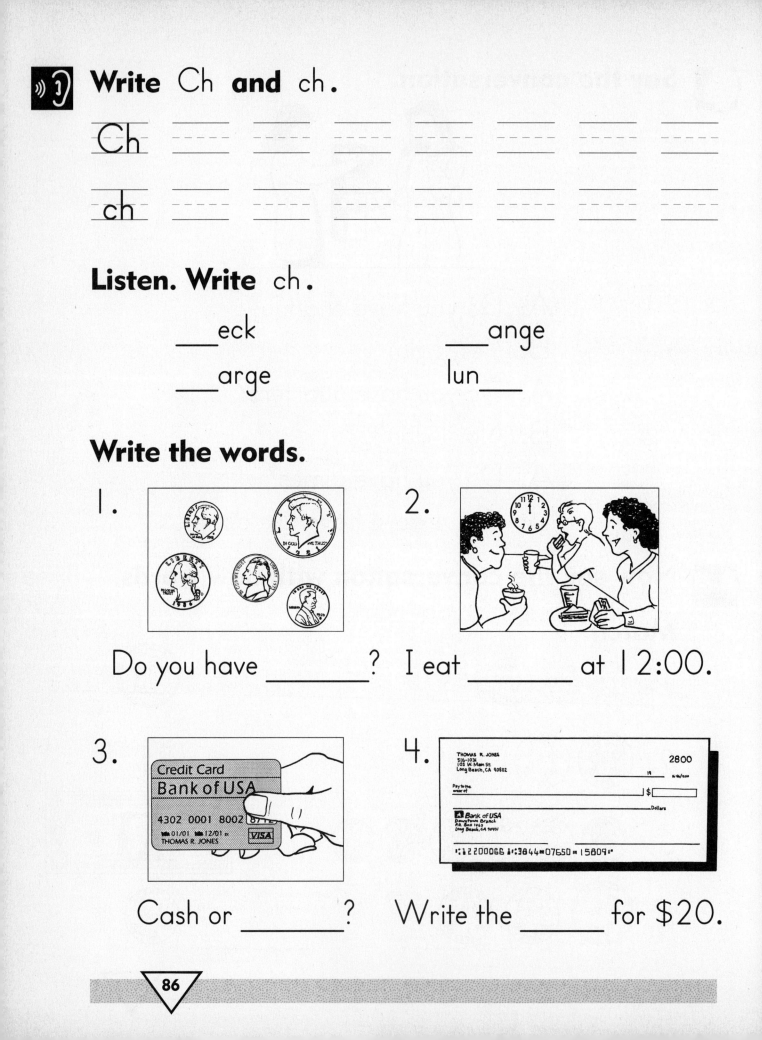

Do you have _____?

2. I eat _____ at 12:00.

3. Cash or _____?

4. Write the _____ for $20.

Say the conversation.

A: May I help you?

B: I want to buy this, please.

A: OK. It's $117.00.

B: Do you take checks?

A: Yes. I need your driver's license.

B: OK. Here you are.

Read and write the words.

ATM card	credit card	driver's license
green card	social security card	

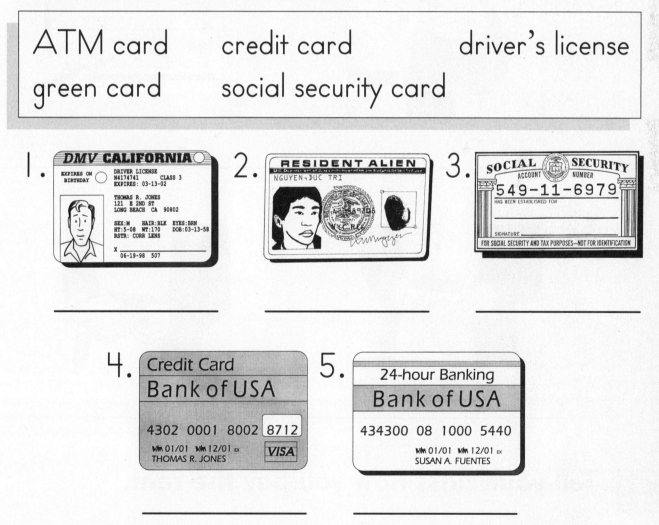

1. DMV CALIFORNIA
EXPIRES ON BIRTHDAY
DRIVER LICENSE
N4174741   CLASS 3
EXPIRES: 03-13-02
THOMAS R. JONES
121 E 2ND ST
LONG BEACH CA 90802
SEX:M HAIR:BLK EYES:BRN
HT:5-08 WT:170 DOB:03-13-58
RSTR: CORR LENS
X
06-19-98 507

_____

2. RESIDENT ALIEN
NGUYEN-DUC TRI

_____

3. SOCIAL SECURITY
ACCOUNT   NUMBER
549-11-6979
HAS BEEN ESTABLISHED FOR
_____
SIGNATURE _____
FOR SOCIAL SECURITY AND TAX PURPOSES—NOT FOR IDENTIFICATION

_____

4. Credit Card
Bank of USA
4302 0001 8002 8712
01/01   12/01 EX
THOMAS R. JONES   VISA

_____

5. 24-hour Banking
Bank of USA
434300 08 1000 5440
01/01   12/01 EX
SUSAN A. FUENTES

_____

Listen. Watch the teacher.

Take out your check.
Write the check.
Show your driver's license.
Show your credit card.

Now you try.

Write the sentences.

1.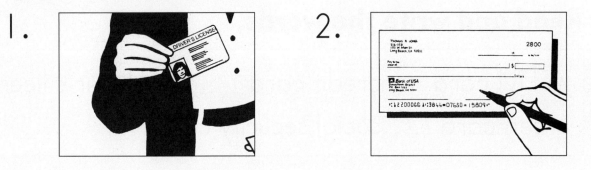

2.

_____

3.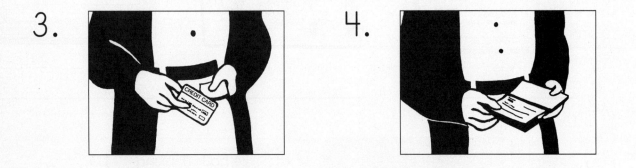

4.

_____

Tell your class how you pay the rent.

Write B and b.

B _ _ _ _ _ _ _

b _ _ _ _ _ _ _

Listen. Write b.

__us   __irthplace

__ank   __irthdate

Write the words.

1. What's your _____?

2. I take the _____.

3. The _____ is open.

4. What's your _____?

A: What's your driver's license number?
B: Sorry. I don't have one.
A: Do you have a social security number?
B: Yes, I do.

Fill out the form.

Name _____

Address _____

City, State, Zip Code _____

_____

Date of Birth _____

Place of Birth _____

Telephone Number ( ) _____

Driver's License Number _____

Social Security Number _____

Credit Card Number _____

Date _____

REVIEW

Read.

1	one	11	eleven	21	twenty-one
2	two	12	twelve	30	thirty
3	three	13	thirteen	40	forty
4	four	14	fourteen	50	fifty
5	five	15	fifteen	60	sixty
6	six	16	sixteen	70	seventy
7	seven	17	seventeen	80	eighty
8	eight	18	eighteen	90	ninety
9	nine	19	nineteen	100	one hundred
10	ten	20	twenty	200	two hundred

Write a check for your telephone bill.

PAY TO _____ $ _____

_____ DOLLARS

Write a check for your rent.

PAY TO _____ $ _____

_____ DOLLARS

93

REVIEW

Ask your classmates.

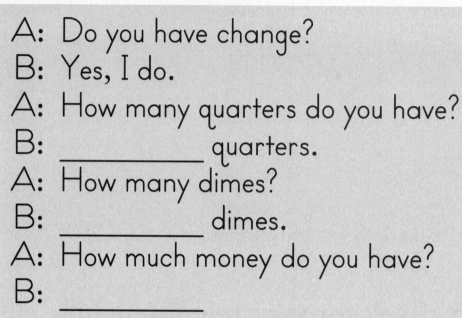

A: Do you have change?
B: Yes, I do.
A: How many quarters do you have?
B: _____ quarters.
A: How many dimes?
B: _____ dimes.
A: How much money do you have?
B: _____

Write the number of quarters, dimes, nickels, and pennies.

Classmate's Name	Quarters	Dimes	Nickels	Pennies

Now talk about your classmates.

I **have** 3 dimes.
Vin **has** 6 dimes and 2 quarters.

Listen.

Say the conversation.

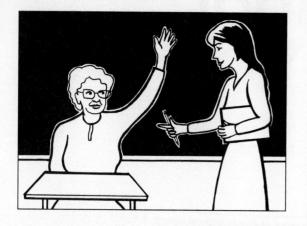

A: Excuse me.
   I need <u>a pencil</u>.
B: OK. Here you are.
A: Thank you very much.
B: You're welcome.

Read and write the words.

| a pencil | an eraser | a book | paper |

1.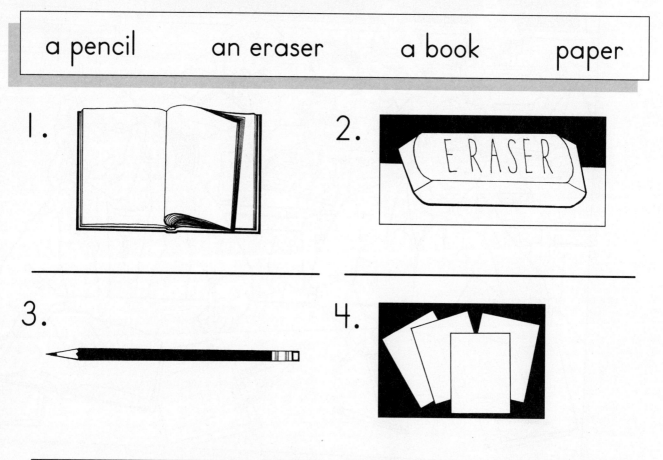
_____

2.
_____

3.
_____

4.
_____

Say the conversation with the new words.

Write P and p.

P _____

p _____

Listen. Write p.

__enny   __encil   slee__

__a__er   sho__ __ing   zi__ code

Write the words.

1. 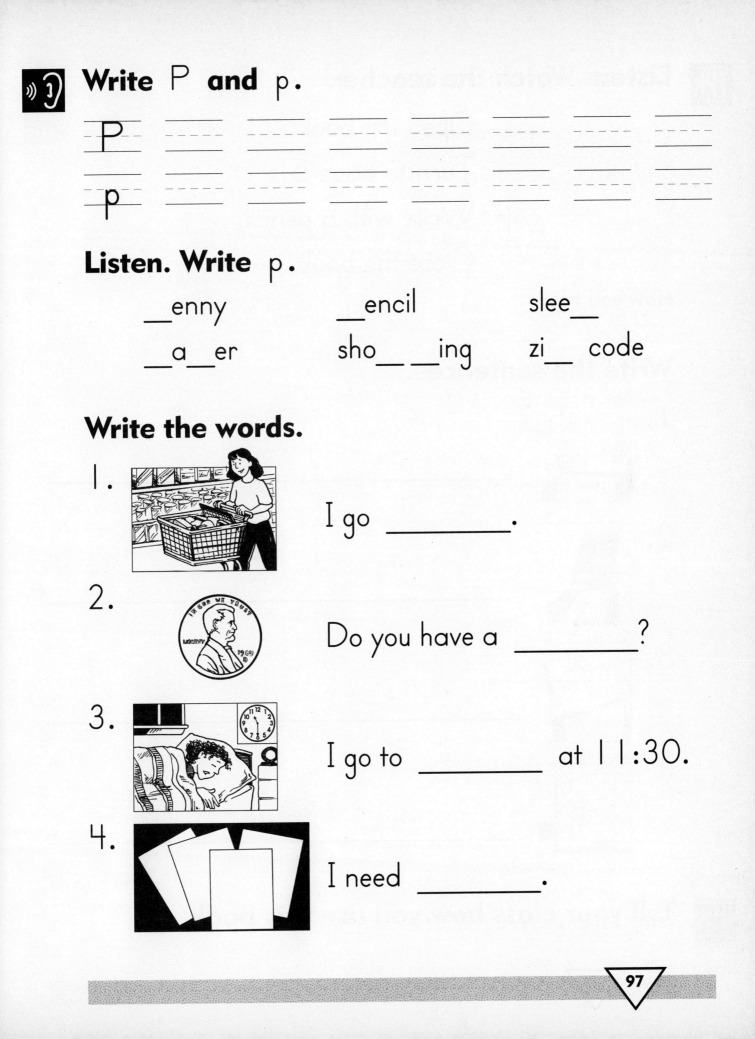 I go _____.

2. Do you have a _____?

3. I go to _____ at 11:30.

4. I need _____.

Listen. Watch the teacher.

Open the book.
Turn to page 5.
Write with a pencil.
Close the book.

Now you try.

Write the sentences.

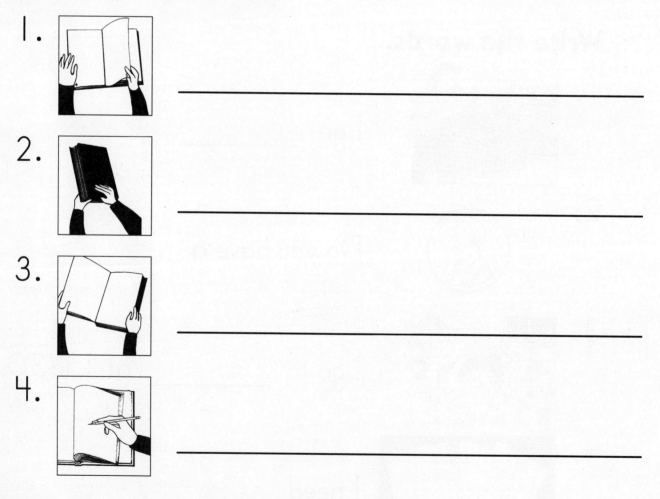

1. _____

2. _____

3. _____

4. _____

Tell your class how you use this book.

Say the conversation.

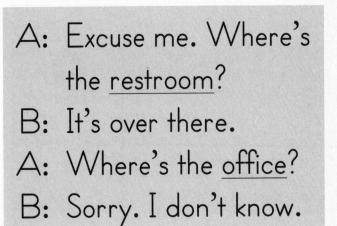

A: Excuse me. Where's the restroom?

B: It's over there.

A: Where's the office?

B: Sorry. I don't know.

Read and write the words.

office	classroom	cafeteria	library

1. _____

2. _____

3. _____

4. _____

Say the conversation with the new words.

Read.

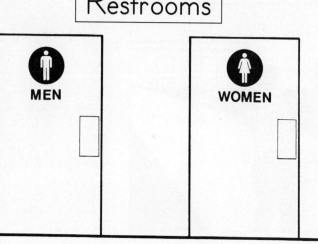

Circle the word.

MEN   WOMEN

MEN   WOMEN

Write.

Walk around the school.
Check Open or Closed.

	Open	Closed
1. Classroom	✔	
2. Cafeteria		
3. Library		
4. Office		
5. Men's Restroom		
6. Women's Restroom		
7.		

Write sentences like this.

1. <u>The classroom is open.</u>
2. _____
3. _____
4. _____
5. _____
6. _____
7. _____

 Tell your class about your school.

C

c

Listen. Write c.

__alendar   __redit __ard   wel__ome

__lassroom   __afeteria   __lose

Write the words.

1. _____ your book.

2. Where's the _____?

3. Do you have a _____ _____?

4. The _____ is open.

Listen to the story.
Write the numbers 1 to 6 for the pictures.

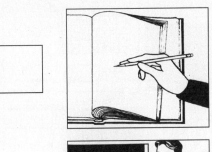

4

1

 Read the story.

Write the story.

1. _____

2. _____

3. _____

4. _____

5. _____

6. _____

Match.

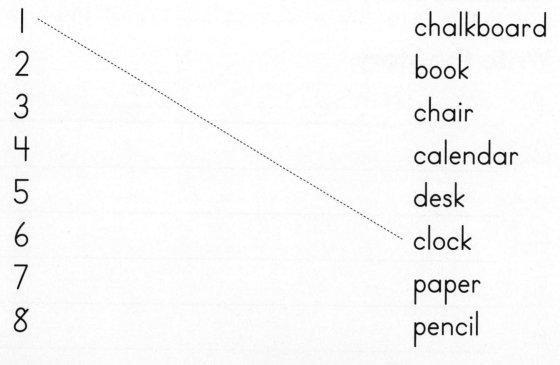

1	chalkboard
2	book
3	chair
4	calendar
5	desk
6	clock
7	paper
8	pencil

Say the conversation.

A: What do you study?
B: I study English.
A: Where?
B: At school.
A: When?
B: In the evening.

 Ask your classmates.

When do you <u>study English</u>?

Write morning, afternoon, **or** evening.

Classmate's Name	Study English	Go to Work	Watch TV

 Talk about your classmates.

David **studies** English in the ____.
Ahmed **goes** to work in the ____.
Sonia **watches** TV in the ____.

Answer the questions. Read the sentences.

1.

What? | Where? | When?
I eat lunch | in the cafeteria | at 12:00.

I eat lunch in the cafeteria at 12:00.

2.

What? | Where? | When?

_____ | _____ | _____

I walk to work in the morning.

3.

What? | Where? | When?

_____ | _____ | _____

I take the bus to the city at 6:00.

 Tell your class about yourself.

Write W and w.

W ‒ ‒ ‒ ‒ ‒ ‒ ‒ ‒ ‒ ‒

w ‒ ‒ ‒ ‒ ‒ ‒ ‒ ‒ ‒ ‒

Listen. Write w.

__ork   __ednesday   __omen   __here

__atch   t__elve   __hat   __hen

Write the words.

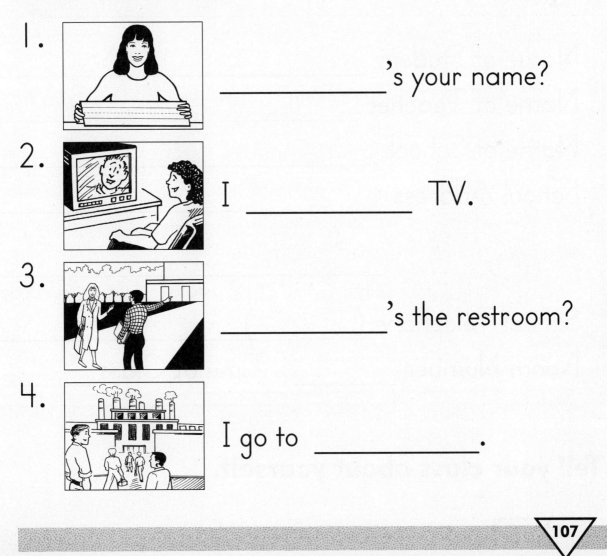

1. _____'s your name?

2. I _____ TV.

3. _____'s the restroom?

4. I go to _____.

Say the conversation.

A: Do you study English?

B: Yes, I do.

A: Where's your class?

B: It's in Room _____.

A: When's your class?

B: At _____.

Fill out the form.

Name of Student _____

Name of Teacher _____

Name of School _____

School Address _____

street

_____

city   state   zip code

School Telephone (___) _____

Room Number _____   Time of Class _____

Tell your class about yourself.

Listen. Write p, c, or w.

1. I __w__alk to the bank on __ednesday.
2. Turn to __age 5.
3. The __lassroom is __losed.
4. I need a __encil and __a__er.
5. Please __ome here.
6. __here's the __omen's restroom?

Find and circle the words.

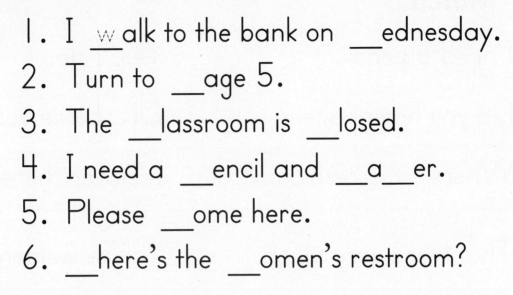

1. men   n e m n e m e n w m e m
2. women   w e n o h e m w o n o w o m e n
3. restroom   s t o m r o s r e s t r o o m o m
4. morning   m o r n g r o n i m o r n i n g n
5. afternoon   t e r a f t e r n o o n t e a f t e r
6. evening   n i n g v n e v e n g e v e n i n g e

Match.

1. I need a pencil. — Yes, I do.

2. Do you have paper? — OK. Here you are.

3. Where's the restroom? It's over there.

---

4. Thank you very much. You're welcome.

5. Where's the office? Yes, I do.

6. Do you study English? Sorry, I don't know.

---

7. What do you study? At school.

8. When? In the evening.

9. Where? I study English.

Choose a question or answer.
Talk to your classmates.
Match questions and answers.

Write nine of the words in the squares.

calendar	clock	pencil	desk	classroom
cafeteria	book	paper	eraser	restroom
library	office	chair	chalkboard	

 Listen. Write an X on the word your teacher says. The student with all Xs wins.

111

Listen.

Say the conversation.

A: Who's he?
B: He's my <u>father</u>.
A: Who's she?
B: She's my <u>mother</u>.

Read and write the words.

mother	wife	daughter
father	husband	son

1. _____

2. _____

3. _____

4. _____

5. _____

6. _____

Read. Circle Yes or No.

1. I live with my mother.   Yes   No

2. I live with my father.   Yes   No

3. I have a wife.   Yes   No

4. I have a husband.   Yes   No

5. I have a son.   Yes   No

6. I have a daughter.   Yes   No

7. I have children.   Yes   No

Write the sentences with Yes circled.

_____

_____

_____

_____

_____

Bring family photographs to class.
Ask about your classmates' photographs.
Talk about your photographs.

 **Say the conversation.**

> A: This is my sister.
> B: Nice to meet you.
> A: This is my brother.
> B: Nice to meet you.

Read. Circle Yes **or** No.

1.	I have one brother.	Yes	No
2.	I have two brothers.	Yes	No
3.	I have _____ brothers. number	Yes	No
4.	I don't have any brothers.	Yes	No
5.	I have one sister.	Yes	No
6.	I have two sisters.	Yes	No
7.	I have _____ sisters. number	Yes	No
8.	I don't have any sisters.	Yes	No

Say the conversation.

> A: How many children do you have?
>
> B: I have <u>two children</u>, <u>one daughter and one son</u>.
>
> A: How many brothers and sisters do you have?
>
> B: I have <u>one brother and two sisters</u>.

Write the answers.

Classmate's Name	Children	Sisters	Brothers

Talk about your classmates.

> I **have** three brothers.
>
> Tina **has** one sister.
>
> Fatima **doesn't have any** children.

Write Th **and** th.

Th ‐ ‐ ‐ ‐ ‐ ‐ ‐ ‐ ‐ ‐
th ‐ ‐ ‐ ‐ ‐ ‐ ‐ ‐ ‐ ‐

Read. Circle the words with th.

A: This is my mother and father.

B: Nice to meet you.

A: This is my brother.

B: Nice to meet you.

Write the words with th.

1. Th _____
2. _____ th _____
3. _____ th _____
4. Th _____
5. _____ th _____

Say the phone conversation.

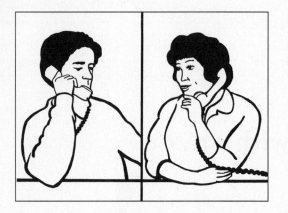

A: Hello.

B: Hello. May I speak to your <u>sister</u>?

A: Sorry. <u>She's</u> not here.

B: What time will she be in?

A: <u>At 6:00.</u>

B: Thank you. Goodbye.

Answer the questions.

1. A: May I speak to your father?

   B: <u>Sorry. He's not here.</u>

2. A: May I speak to your wife?

   B: _____

3. A: May I speak to your son?

   B: _____

4. A: May I speak to your husband?

   B: _____

Now say the conversation with a classmate.

Say the phone conversation.

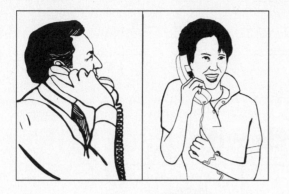

A: Hello.
B: Hello. May I speak to your <u>brother</u>?
A: <u>Just a minute, please.</u>
B: <u>Thank you.</u>

Answer the questions.

1. A: May I speak to your mother?
   B: <u>Just a minute, please.</u>

2. A: May I speak to your daughter?
   B: <u>Sorry. She's not here.</u>

3. A: May I speak to your son?
   B: <u>Just</u>

4. A: May I speak to your father?
   B: <u>Sorry</u>

5. A: May I speak to your wife?
   B: <u>Just</u>

Now say the conversation with a classmate.

Write H and h.

H — — — — — — — — — — — — — — — —

h — — — — — — — — — — — — — — — —

Read. Circle the words with h.

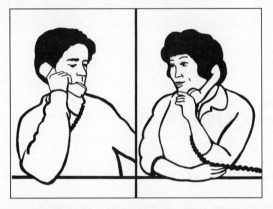

A: Hello. How are you?

B: I'm fine, thank you.

A: May I speak to your husband?

B: Sorry. He's not here.

A: When will he be in?

B: He'll be home at 6:30.

Write the words with h.

1. H _____

2. H _____

3.   h _____

4. h _____

5. H _____

6.   h _____

7.   h _____

8. h _____

9. H _____

10. h _____

Listen. Watch the teacher.

Pick up the receiver.

Dial the phone number.

Talk on the phone.

Hang up.

Now you try.

Write the sentences.

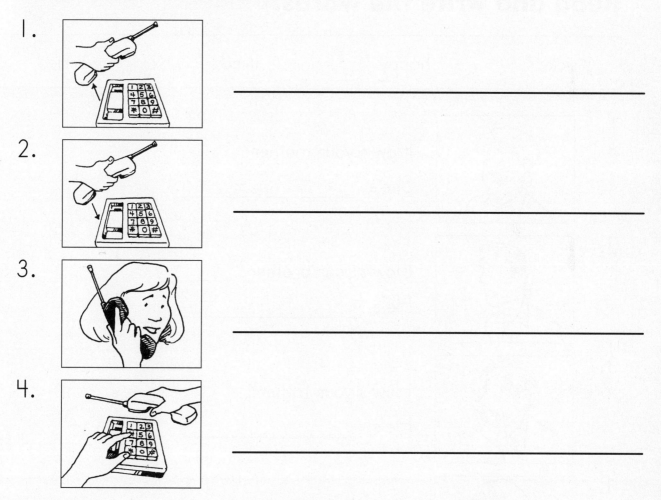

1. _____

2. _____

3. _____

4. _____

Language Experience # Tell your class how you use a pay phone.

Say the conversation.

A: Hello. How are you?

B: Fine, thank you.

A: How's your sister?

B: She's <u>busy</u>.

She has two jobs.

Read and write the words.

| sick | happy | tired | worried |

1. How's your mother?

   She's _____.

2. How's your brother?

   He's _____.

3. How's your father?

   He's _____.

4. How's your daughter?

   She's _____.

Match.

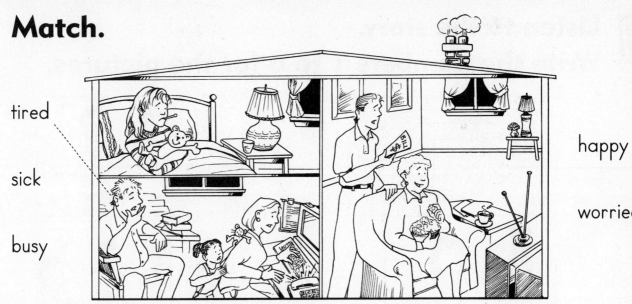

tired

sick

busy

happy

worried

 ## Ask your classmates.

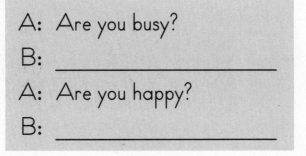

A: Are you busy?

B: _____

A: Are you happy?

B: _____

Write yes or no.

Classmate's Name	Busy	Happy	Sick	Tired	Worried

Talk about your classmates.

Listen to the story.
Write the numbers 1 to 6 for the pictures.

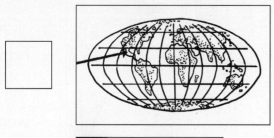

[ ] □ 1

[ ] □

[4] □

 Read the story.

Write the story.

1. _____

2. _____

3. _____

4. _____

5. _____

6. _____

Complete your story.
Tell your story to a classmate.

1. I'm _____.
   name

2. I'm from _____.
   birthplace

3. I'm _____ years old.
   age

4. I _____ every day.

5. I'm a good _____.

6. I'm very _____.

Write your classmate's story.

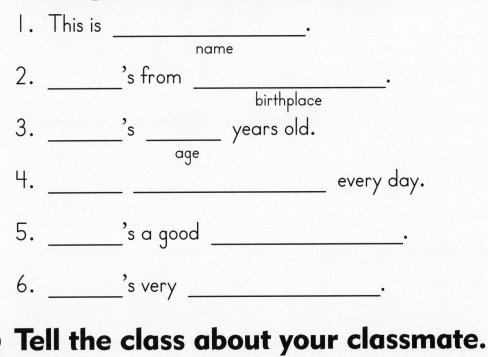

1. This is _____.
   name

2. _____'s from _____.
   birthplace

3. _____'s _____ years old.
   age

4. _____ _____ every day.

5. _____'s a good _____.

6. _____'s very _____.

Tell the class about your classmate.

Fill out the form.

_____   _____   _____
First Name   Middle Name   Last Name

Birthplace _____   Birthdate _____

Age _____   Sex ☐ F
                             ☐ M

Husband/Wife's Name _____

Children's Names   Ages

_____   _____

_____   _____

_____   _____

_____   _____

Father's Name _____

Mother's Name _____

Number of Brothers _____

Number of Sisters _____

REVIEW

Match.

1. Who's he?   I don't have any children.

2. How many sisters do you have?   He's my father.

3. How many children do you have?   I have two sisters.

---

4. This is my brother.   Sorry. She's not here.

5. May I speak to your mother?   Nice to meet you.

6. May I speak to your son?   Just a minute, please.

---

7. How are you?   Fine, thank you.

8. How's your husband?   Hello.

9. Hello.   He's busy.

Choose a question or answer.
Talk to your classmates.
Match questions and answers.

Write nine of the words in the squares.

wife	children	mother	brothers	sisters
sons	sister	husband	daughters	
father	daughter	son	brother	

Listen. Write an X on the word your teacher says. The student with all Xs wins.

Listen.

1.29/lb.   1.39/lb.   .99/lb.   1.19/lb.

Say the conversation.

A: May I help you?

B: What's in the fruit salad?

A: Oranges, pears, apples, and bananas.

B: OK. I want the fruit salad.

Circle the word.

1. (apple)
   orange

2. peach
   banana

3. orange
   lemon

4. pear
   apple

5. pineapple
   lemon

6. apple
   peach

7. pineapple
   banana

8. fruits
   coffee

Write the word for two or more.

1. 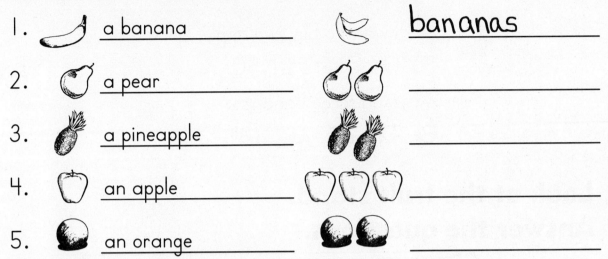 a banana   bananas

2. a pear _____

3. a pineapple _____

4. an apple _____

5. an orange _____

 ## Ask your classmates.

> A: What fruits do you like?
>
> B: I like _____.
>
> A: Do you like bananas?
>
> B: _____

Write the answers.

Classmate's Name	Like	Don't Like

 ## Talk about your classmates.

Pedro **likes** apples.   Sami **doesn't like** bananas.

Say the conversation.

> A: I want to buy <u>two apples</u>, please.
> B: OK. That's <u>$1.50</u>.
> A: And <u>three bananas</u>.
> B: That's <u>$3.00</u> in all.

Look at the fruit stand.
Answer the questions.

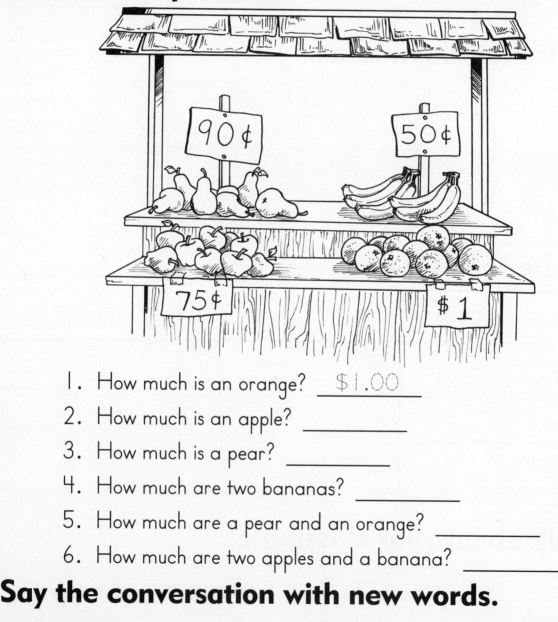

1. How much is an orange? <u>$1.00</u>
2. How much is an apple? _____
3. How much is a pear? _____
4. How much are two bananas? _____
5. How much are a pear and an orange? _____
6. How much are two apples and a banana? _____

Say the conversation with new words.

Say the conversation.

A: May I help you?

B: I want a hamburger.

A: With lettuce, tomatoes, and onions?

B: I want lettuce and tomatoes, but no onions.

A: Anything else?

B: No, thanks.

Circle the word.

1. (carrot) / potato	2. pepper / onion
3. potato / mushroom	4. potato / tomato
5. fruit / pepper	6. mushroom / carrot
7. lettuce / tomato	8. fruits / vegetables

Write the word for two or more.

1. a pepper   _peppers_

2. a carrot

3. an onion

4. a potato

5. a tomato

Ask your classmates.

A: What vegetables do you like?

B: I like _____.

A: Do you like mushrooms?

B: _____

Write the answers.

Classmate's Name	Like	Don't Like

Talk about your classmates.

Maria **likes** onions.   Nick **doesn't like** onions.

Look at the vegetables.
Answer the questions.

Signs on display:
- MUSHROOMS $1.79/lb.
- TOMATOES $2.39/lb.
- POTATOES 99¢/lb.
- ONIONS 79¢/lb.

1. How much are onions? _79¢ a pound_____
2. How much are mushrooms? _____
3. How much are potatoes? _____
4. How much are tomatoes? _____

Write is or are.

1. How much ___is___ a pear?
2. How much ___are___ potatoes?
3. How much _____ apples?
4. How much _____ a tomato?
5. How much _____ onions?
6. How much _____ oranges?
7. How much _____ a banana?
8. How much _____ a potato?

Listen to the story.
Write the numbers 1 to 6 for the pictures.

Read the story.

Write the story.

1. _____

2. _____

3. _____

4. _____

5. _____

6. _____

Check what you like for breakfast.

- ☐ soup
- ☐ eggs
- ☐ fruit
- ☐ donut
- ☐ cereal
- ☐ _____

Check what you like for lunch.

- ☐ noodles
- ☐ hamburger
- ☐ sandwich
- ☐ salad
- ☐ pizza
- ☐ _____

Check what you like for dinner.

- ☐ rice
- ☐ vegetables
- ☐ fish
- ☐ steak
- ☐ chicken
- ☐ _____

Check what you like to drink.

- ☐ tea
- ☐ coffee
- ☐ milk
- ☐ soda
- ☐ juice
- ☐ _____

Ask your classmates.

> A: What do you like to eat?
>
> B: I like _____.
>
> A: Anything else?
>
> B: _____
>
> A: What do you like to drink?
>
> B: _____

Write the food and drinks.

Classmate's Name	Eat	Drink

Write sentences like this.

1. _____ likes to eat _____ and drink _____.
        name

2. _____

3. _____

4. _____

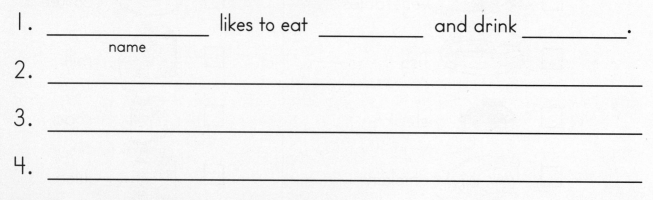 ## Talk about your classmates.

Write Sh **and** sh.

Sh ___ ___ ___ ___ ___ ___ ___

sh ___ ___ ___ ___ ___ ___ ___

Listen. Write sh.

____e   wa____

____opping   ca____

____ow   Engli____

Write the words.

1. _____ likes to go _____ .
2. _____ or charge?
3. I study _____ .
4. I _____ the apple and eat it.
5. _____ me your driver's license.

Listen. Write sh **or** ch.

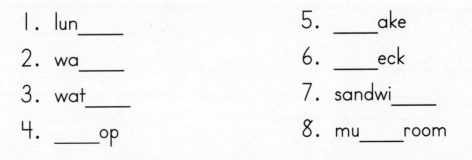

1. lun____   5. ____ake

2. wa____   6. ____eck

3. wat____   7. sandwi____

4. ____op   8. mu____room

Go to the cafeteria, restaurant, or coffee truck.
Look at the menu. Write the price.

FOODS

1. Hamburger $ _____
2. Salad   _____
3. Chicken   _____
4. Sandwich   _____
5. Donut   _____
6. _____   _____
7. _____   _____
8. _____   _____

DRINKS

9. Coffee $ _____
10. Tea   _____
11. Juice   _____
12. Milk   _____
13. Soda   _____
14. _____   _____

Match.

1. Do you like pineapples?   Oranges, apples, and bananas.

2. How much is a pear?   It's 35¢.

3. What's in the fruit salad?   Yes, I do.

---

4. May I help you?   I want a hamburger.

5. What vegetables do you like?   Yes, please.

6. Do you want onions?   I like potatoes.

---

7. What do you like to drink?   I like chicken.

8. Anything else?   No, thanks.

9. What do you like to eat?   I like coffee.

Choose a question or answer.
Talk to your classmates.
Match questions and answers.

REVIEW

Write the words under fruits, vegetables, drinks, or food.

Fruits	Vegetables	Drinks	Food
			chicken

apple	lemon	potato
banana	lettuce	rice
carrot	milk	sandwich
✓ chicken	noodles	soda
coffee	onion	soup
fish	orange	tea
hamburger	peach	tomato
juice	pizza	

Listen.

Teacher's Resource Book

POLICE

AMBULANCE

FIRE

Say the conversation.

 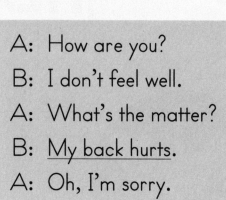

A: How are you?
B: I don't feel well.
A: What's the matter?
B: My back hurts.
A: Oh, I'm sorry.

Read the words.

| neck | chest | arm | leg |

Write the sentences.

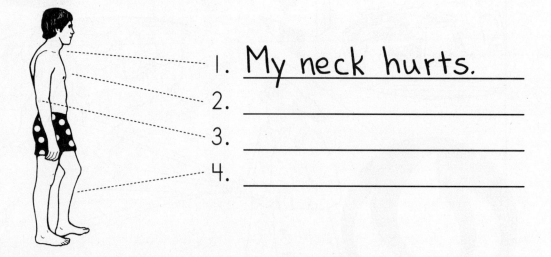

1. My neck hurts.
2. _____
3. _____
4. _____

 Say the conversation with the new words.

Listen. Watch your teacher. Write the words.

mouth   eye

neck   head

ear   nose

_____

stomach   chest

arm   hand

finger   shoulder

_____

foot   knee

toe   hip

leg   ankle

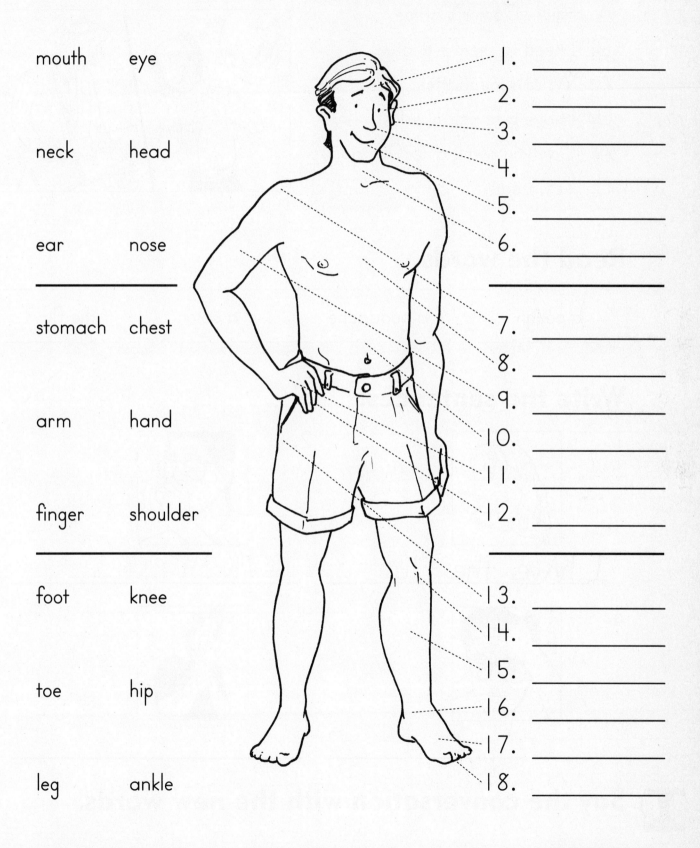

1. _____
2. _____
3. _____
4. _____
5. _____
6. _____

7. _____
8. _____
9. _____
10. _____
11. _____
12. _____

13. _____
14. _____
15. _____
16. _____
17. _____
18. _____

🗣 Say the conversation.

A: Hello. Doctor's office.

B: I need to see the doctor.

A: What's the matter?

B: I have <u>a fever</u>.

A: Can you come at 3:00 today?

B: Yes, I can.

Read the words.

a cough	a headache	a cold	the flu

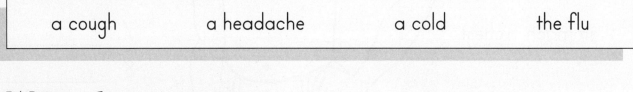

Write the sentences.

1. <u>I have the flu.</u>

2. _____

3. _____

4. _____

👥 Say the conversation with the new words.

Write M and m.

M ------------------------------

m ------------------------------

Read. Circle the words with m.

A: May I help you?
B: I need to see the doctor.
A: What's the matter?
B: My arm hurts.

Write the words with m.

1. M _____
2. m _____

3. M _____
4. _____ m

Listen. Write m or n.

1. ___onth
2. ___ose
3. ___eed

4. ___outh
5. k___ee
6. ___oney

Match.

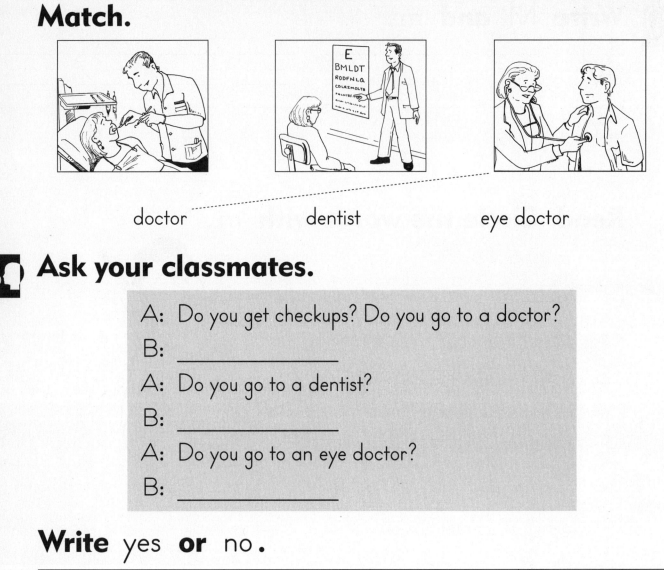

doctor   dentist   eye doctor

Ask your classmates.

A: Do you get checkups? Do you go to a doctor?

B: _____

A: Do you go to a dentist?

B: _____

A: Do you go to an eye doctor?

B: _____

Write yes **or** no.

Classmate's Name	Doctor	Dentist	Eye Doctor

Talk about your classmates.

Wan Li **goes** to a dentist.   Vicki **doesn't go** to a dentist.

Listen. Watch the teacher.

Sit on the table.

Open your mouth. Say ahh.

Breathe in. Breathe out.

Lie down.

Now you try.

Write the sentences.

1.

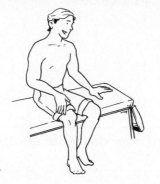

_____

_____

2.

_____

_____

3.

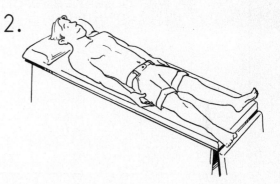

_____

_____

4.

_____

_____

Language Experience # Tell your class what you do at the doctor's office.

Write to your child's teacher.

_____
date

Dear _____,
teacher's name

    Please excuse my son _____.
son's name

He was absent yesterday because he had a cold.

              Sincerely,

_____
mother or father's name

_____
date

Dear _____,
teacher's name

    Please excuse my daughter _____.
daughter's name

She was absent yesterday because she had a fever.

              Sincerely,

_____
mother or father's name

Write F and f.

F — — — — — — — — — —
f — — — — — — — — — —

Read. Circle the words with f.

A: How are you?
B: Fine, thank you.
A: How's your family?
B: My father's sick.
A: What's the matter?
B: He has the flu.

Write the words with f.

1. F _____   3. f _____
2. f _____   4. f _____

Listen. Write f or v.

1. ___ever   4. co___ ___ee
2. ___ery   5. ___oot
3. ___egetable   6. ha___e

Listen to the story.
Write the numbers 1 to 6 for the pictures.

☐

☐

☐

☐ 1

5

☐

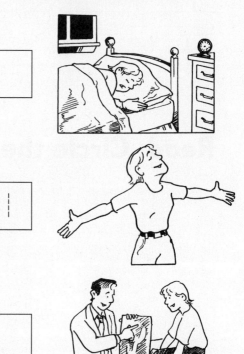

 Read the story.

Write the story.

1. _____
2. _____
3. _____
4. _____
5. _____
6. _____

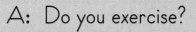

Ask your classmates.

A: Do you exercise?

B: _____

A: Do you smoke?

B: _____

A: Do you have any problems?

B: <u>Sometimes my back hurts.</u>

Write the answers.

Classmate's Name	Exercise	Smoke	Problems

 # Ask your class the questions.
Count the students.

1. How many students exercise? _____
   number

2. How many students eat fruits and vegetables? _____

3. How many students get checkups? _____

4. How many students smoke? _____

5. How many students sleep seven hours? _____

Say the conversation.

A: 911. Emergency.

B: Help! My friend needs an ambulance.

A: What's the matter?

B: He can't breathe.

A: Where are you?

B: The address is _____ .

Read and write the sentences.

He can't get up.	He's unconscious.
He's bleeding.	His chest hurts.

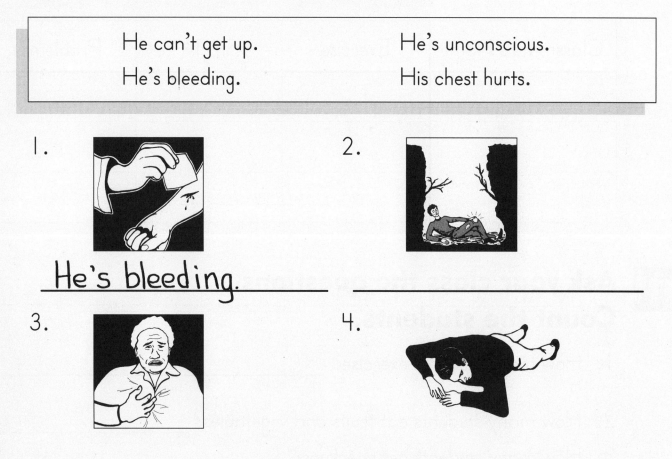

1.

He's bleeding.

2.

3.

4.

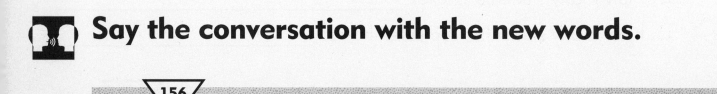 **Say the conversation with the new words.**

Say the conversation.

A: 911. Emergency.

B: Help! I need the police.

A: What happened?

B: My <u>money</u> was stolen.

A: Where are you?

B: I'm at _____.

Read the words.

| wallet | watch | car | purse |

Write the sentences.

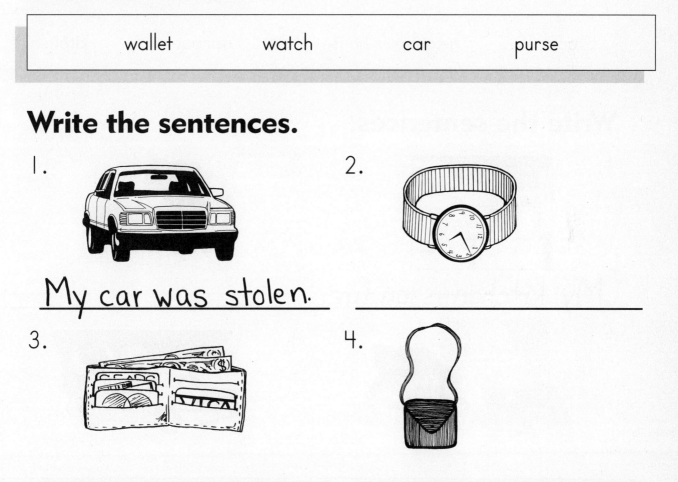

1.

My car was stolen.

2.

3.

4.

Say the conversation with the new words.

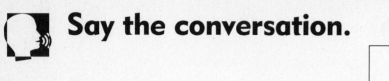 **Say the conversation.**

A: 911. Emergency.

B: Help! My <u>house</u> is on fire.

A: What's your address?

B: My address is _____.

Read the words.

| car | neighbor's house | garage | kitchen |

Write the sentences.

1.

My kitchen is on fire.

2.

_____

3.

_____

4.

_____

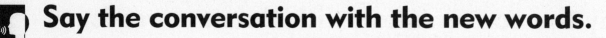 **Say the conversation with the new words.**

Match.

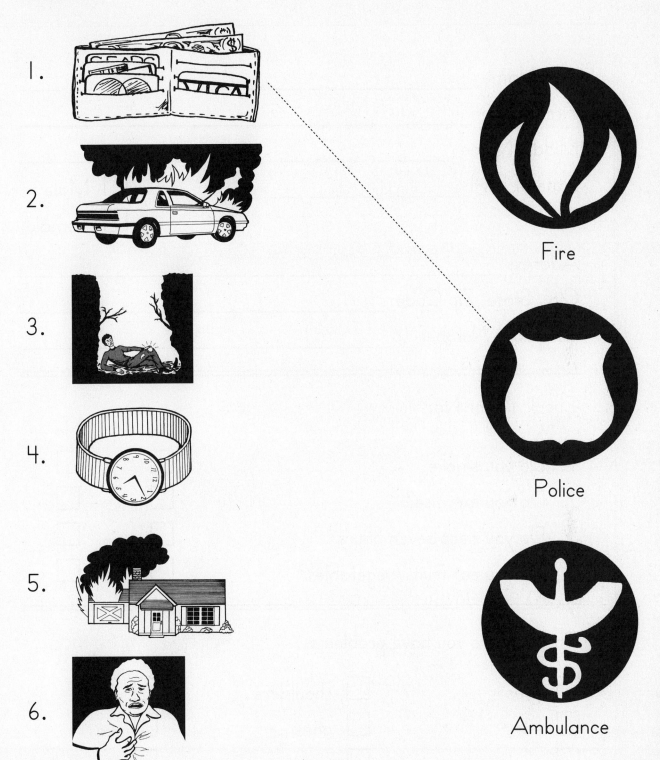

1.

2.

3.

4.

5.

6.

Fire

Police

Ambulance

With a classmate, say the telephone conversation for each picture.

Fill out the form.

Last Name _____

First Name _____

Middle Name _____

Date of Birth _____   ☐ Male
                                    ☐ Female

Address _____

City, State, Zip Code _____

Telephone Number (_____) _____

Check Yes or No.

	Yes	No
1. Do you smoke?	☐	☐
2. Do you exercise?	☐	☐
3. Do you sleep seven hours?	☐	☐
4. Do you eat fruits/vegetables?	☐	☐

Check where you have problems.

☐ eyes   ☐ shoulders   ☐ hips

☐ ears   ☐ chest   ☐ legs

☐ neck   ☐ arms   ☐ knees

☐ back   ☐ stomach   ☐ ankles

REVIEW

Match.

1. How are you?   My back hurts.

2. What's the matter?   Yes, I do.

3. Do you get checkups?   I don't feel well.

---

4. What's your address?   Help! I need the police.

5. 911. Emergency.   My address is _____.

6. What happened?   My money was stolen.

---

7. What's the matter?   My chest hurts.

8. Do you smoke?   Yes. I walk to school.

9. Do you exercise?   No, I don't.

**Choose a question or answer.
Talk to your classmates.
Match questions and answers.**

Write nine of the words in the squares.

stomach	hand	eye	leg	head
back	ankle	shoulder	arm	ear
chest	mouth	neck	knee	foot

Listen. Write an ✕ on the word your teacher says. The student with all ✕s wins.

 ## Listen.

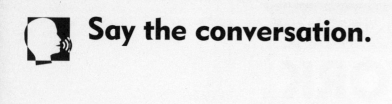

Say the conversation.

A: Do you have a job?
B: Yes, I do.
A: What do you do?
B: I'm a <u>restaurant</u> worker.

Read the words.

| office | hospital | factory | garment |

Write the sentences.

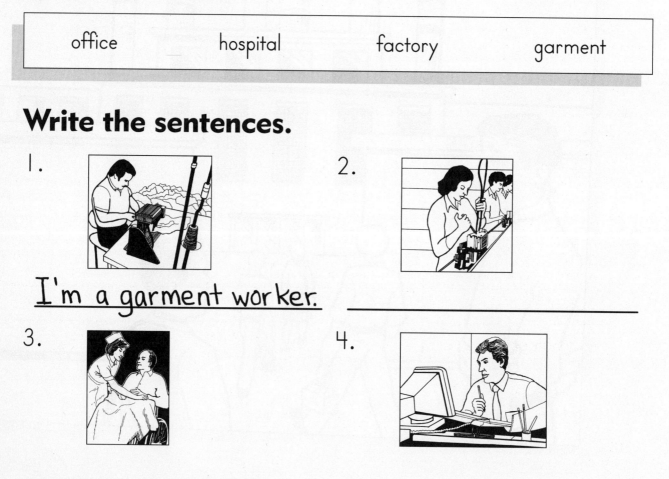

1.

I'm a garment worker.

2.

3.

4.

Say the conversation with the new words.

Match.

sales clerk   mechanic   teacher   bus driver

 ## Ask your classmates.

A: Do you want to be a <u>sales clerk</u>?

B: _____

A: Do you want to be a <u>mechanic</u>?

B: _____

Write yes, no, or maybe.

Job	Classmate 1	Classmate 2	Classmate 3
restaurant worker			
garment worker			
hospital worker			
factory worker			
office worker			
sales clerk			
mechanic			
teacher			
bus driver			

 # Talk about your classmates.

George **wants to be** a teacher.   Frank, Lisa, and Ming **want to be** sales clerks.

Write the capital letters.

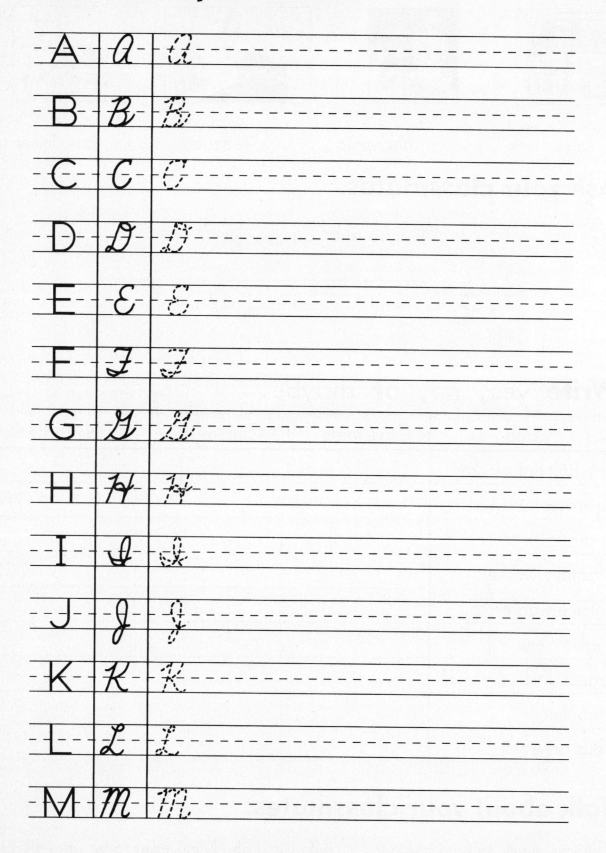

Write the capital letters.

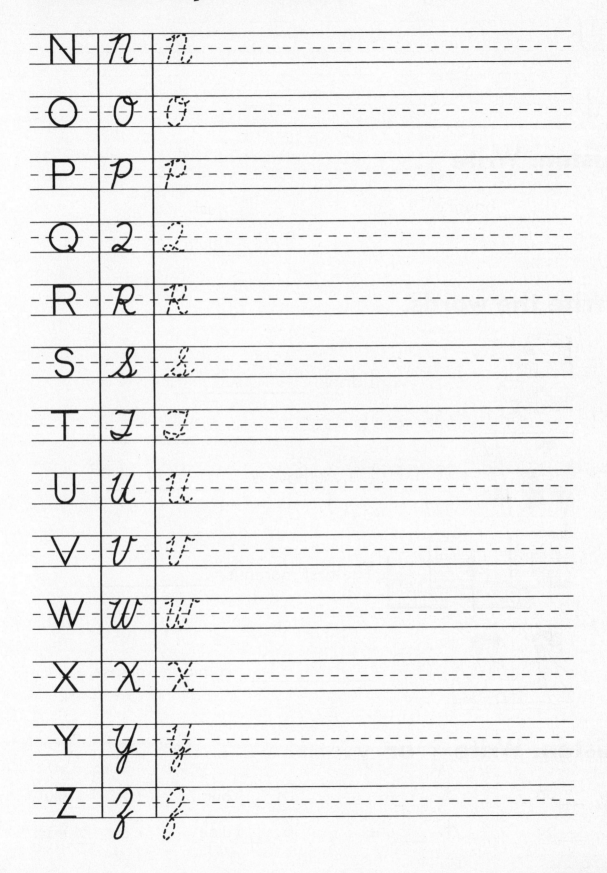

Write J and j.

J __ __ __ __ __ __

j __ __ __ __ __ __

Listen. Write j.

___anuary

___ob

___ust

___uice

Write the words.

1. I drink _____.

2. Do you have a _____?

3. The first month is _____.

4. _____ a minute, please.

Listen. Write j or y.

1. ___ob

2. ___ou

3. ___es

4. ___une

5. ___our

6. ___uice

7. ___uly

8. ___ear

Listen. Watch the teacher.

Take the box to the table.

Put the box down.

Pick the box up.

Give the box to the customer.

Now you try.

Write the sentences.

1.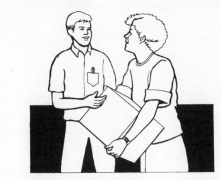

_____

_____

2.

_____

_____

3.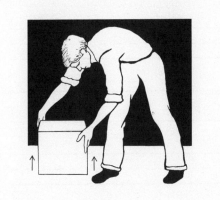

_____

_____

4.

_____

_____

Language Experience # Tell your class what you do at work.

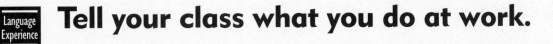

Write the small letters.

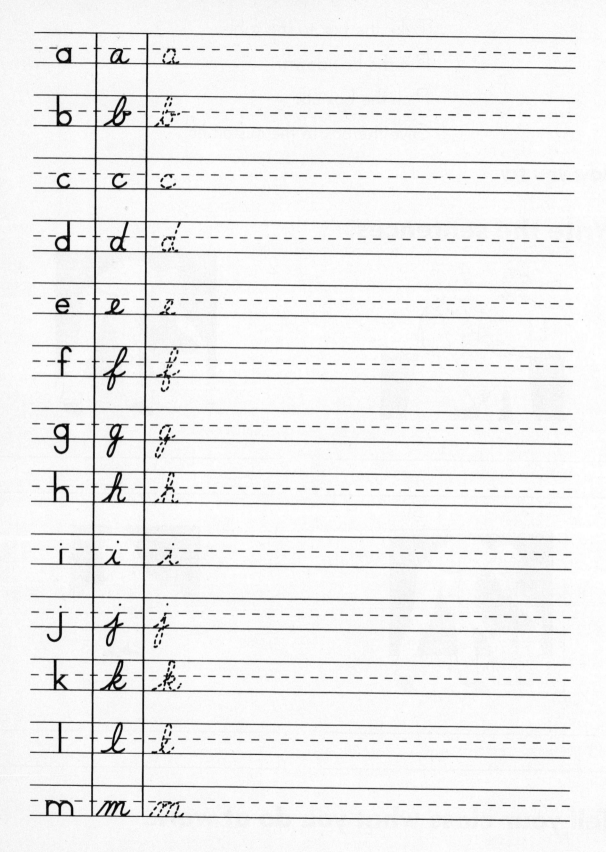

Write the small letters.

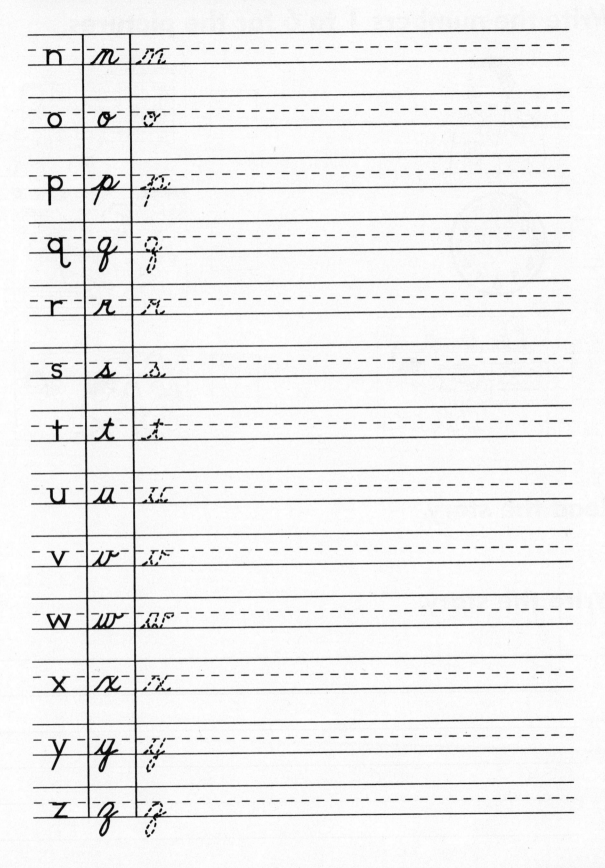

Listen to the story.
Write the numbers 1 to 6 for the pictures.

| 1 | | |  |

| |  | 2 | |

| |  | | |

Read the story.

Write the story.

1. _____

2. _____

3. _____

4. _____

5. _____

6. _____

Read the time card.

ABC Company

Employee __John Lee__   Date __April 1-7__

	In	Lunch Out	Lunch In	Out	Total Hours
Sun.					
Mon.	8:00	12:00	1:00	5:00	8
Tues.	8:00	12:00	1:00	5:00	8
Wed.	8:00	12:00	1:00	5:00	8
Thurs.	8:00	12:00	1:00	5:00	8
Fri.	8:00	12:00	1:00	5:00	8
Sat.					
				Total Hours for Week	40

Write Yes, he does., No, he doesn't., **or** I don't know.

1. Does John work on Friday? _____

2. Does he go to work at 12:00? _____

3. Does he go to school at 6:00? _____

4. Does he eat lunch at home? _____

5. Does he work 8 hours a week? _____

6. Does he work 5 days a week? _____

Write a story about John Lee.

John Lee goes to work at 8:00.

Fill out your time card.

	In	Lunch Out	Lunch In	Out	Total Hours
Company _____					
Employee _____		Date _____			
Sun.					
Mon.					
Tues.					
Wed.					
Thurs.					
Fri.					
Sat.					
				Total Hours for Week	

Answer the questions.

1. Do you work Monday to Friday? _____

2. What time do you go to work? _____

3. What time do you eat lunch? _____

4. What time do you go home? _____

5. How many hours do you work in one day? _____

6. How many hours do you work in one week? _____

Now ask a classmate.

Write a story about your classmate.

Write the capital and small letters.

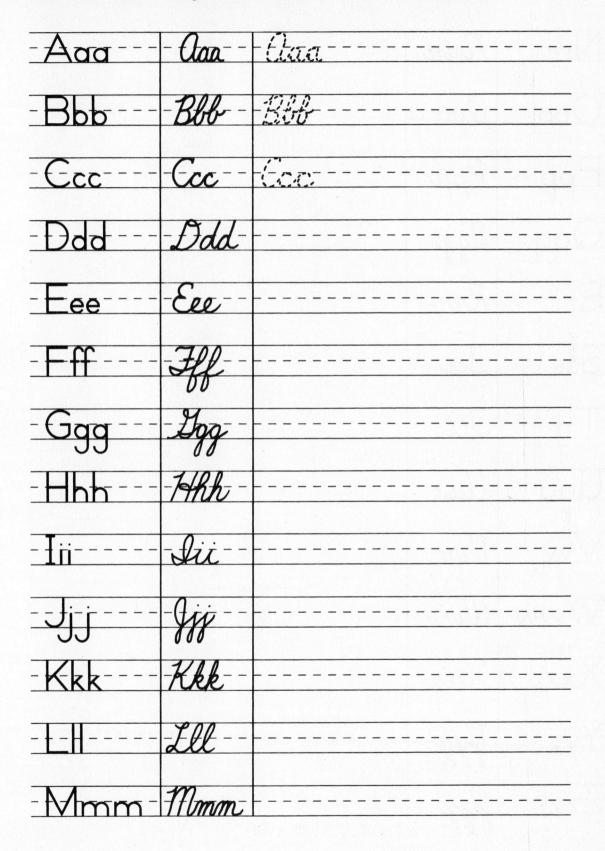

Write the capital and small letters.

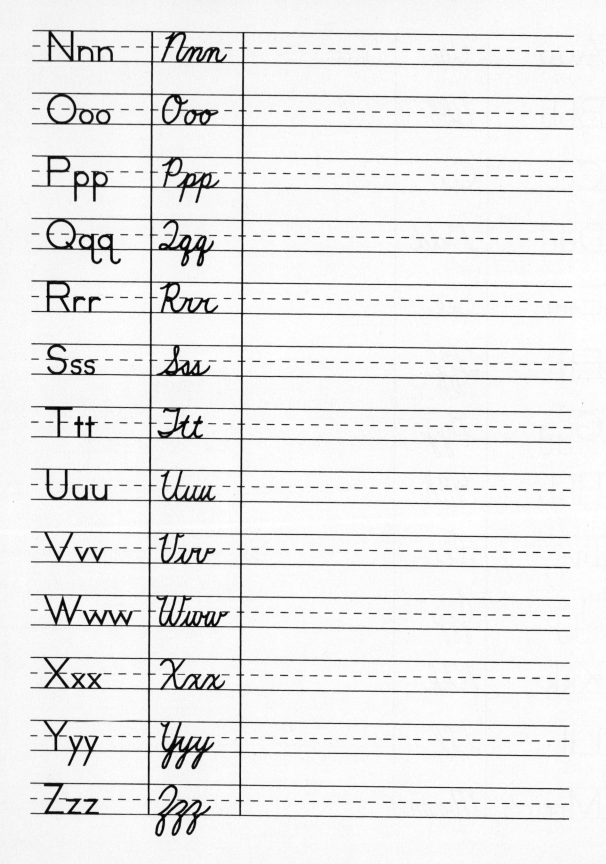

Nnn   Nnn

Ooo   Ooo

Ppp   Ppp

Qqq   Qqq

Rrr   Rrr

Sss   Sss

Ttt   Ttt

Uuu   Uuu

Vvv   Vvv

Www   Www

Xxx   Xxx

Yyy   Yyy

Zzz   Zzz

Say the conversation.

A: I want to apply for a job.

B: Do you have experience?

A: Yes. I was a restaurant worker.

B: Where?

A: At ABC Restaurant in Los Angeles.

B: For how long?

A: Two years.

Read the form.

Work Experience

Company __ABC Restaurant__

Address __100 Sunset St., Los Angeles__

Job __Restaurant Worker__

Date: From _1995_   To _1997_

Fill out the form.

Work Experience

Company _____

Address _____

Job _____

Date: From _____   To _____

🗣️ Ask your classmates.

A: Do you have work experience?

B: Yes. I was a _____.

A: Where?

B: _____

A: For how long?

B: _____

Write the answers.

Classmate's Name	Experience	Where	How Long

Write sentences like this.

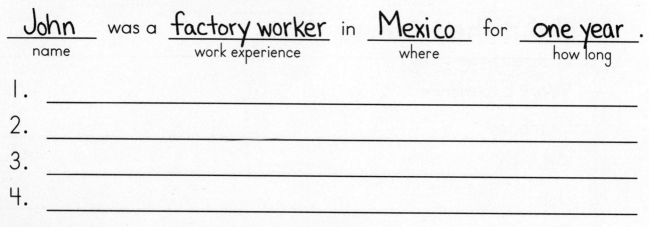

__John__ was a __factory worker__ in __Mexico__ for __one year__ .
name   work experience   where   how long

1. _____
2. _____
3. _____
4. _____

🗣️ Talk about your classmates.

Write R and r.

R R R R R R R R R

r r r r r r r r

Listen. Write r.

__est__oom   custome__

__estau__ant   fi__e

Write the words.

1. Give the box to the _____.

2. Excuse me. Where's the _____?

3. I'm a _____ worker.

4. Help! My house is on _____.

Listen. Write r or l.

1. __ead   3. worke__   5. schoo__   7. d__ink

2. __ook   4. __ike   6. w__ite   8. __ong

Say the conversation.

A: May I help you?
B: I want to apply for a job.
A: Please fill out the application.
B: OK.
A: Please sign your name here.
B: OK. Thank you.

Write your signature.

Write.

Print your name. _____
                       first   last

Sign your name. _____

Write your signature. _____

Fill out the application.

Date _____

Name _____ _____ _____
                   last   first   middle

Address _____
                                    street

_____ _____ _____
            city   state   zip code

Telephone (_____) _____

Social Security No. _____

___

Work Experience

Company _____

    Address _____

    Telephone _____

Job _____

Date: From _____   To _____

___

Work Experience

Company _____

    Address _____

    Telephone _____

Job _____

Date: From _____   To _____

___

Signature _____

Match.

1. Do you have a job?   Eight hours a day.

2. What do you do?   I'm a sales clerk.

3. How many hours do you work?   Yes, I do.

---

4. Do you work Monday to Friday?   12:00.

5. What time do you go to work?   Yes, I do.

6. What time do you eat lunch?   8:00.

---

7. Do you have experience?   At ABC Factory.

8. Where?   Yes. I was a factory worker.

9. For how long?   Two years.

Choose a question or answer.
Talk to your classmates.
Match questions and answers.

 **Ask your classmates.**

A: What's your last name?

B: _____

A: Please sign your name here.

B: OK.

Write your classmates' last names.

Last Names A to F	Last Names G to L
_____	_____
_____	_____
_____	_____
_____	_____
_____	_____
_____	_____

Last Names M to S	Last Names T to Z
_____	_____
_____	_____
_____	_____
_____	_____
_____	_____
_____	_____